GET[ ]
AWAY
WITH
MURDER

A TRUE STORY

Eira

ISBN 978-1-68526-046-0 (Paperback)
ISBN 978-1-68526-047-7 (Digital)

Covenant Books, Inc.
11661 Hwy 707
Murrells Inlet, SC 29576
www.covenantbooks.com

Dedicated to my mentally challenged Aunt Vimla, who remained unrecognized and invisible until blamed for a murder.

ACKNOWLEDGMENTS

My heartfelt thanks to Sushma Goel, who fed and housed me and to her sister, Shashi Gupta, for her unceasing goodwill and encouragement. My thanks to Rajiv Prasad for contributing precious photographs of the family.

My gratitude to the members of the reference desk of Transylvania County Library, especially to Susan Chambers and Martha Snow, for their technical computer assistance.

Without the help of the above, this memoir would never have seen the light of day.

CONTENTS

INTRODUCTION

"Every man is an omnibus in which his ancestor's ride" (Oliver Wendell Holmes). I was born and raised in a *Brahmin* family (reputedly the highest caste in India) in Uttar Pradesh, India. Although both my parents were committed to the Hindu way of life, they had a deep appreciation and a keen fascination with Western civilization as reflected in the British imperialist, quasi humanist, colonial endeavor. Thus the family was a contradiction, Western and Eastern, traditional and modern simultaneously. It was in the likeness of a hybrid tree with two contrasting trunks entwined or of a face that is sharply divided by a line through the middle, dividing it into two half semicircles: half brown and half white.

As a traditional Brahman family, it was imperative that the family reputation remain unsmirched by any scandal. We were expected to be as pure as the driven snow. Our friends were carefully screened as was any prospective son-in-law. But as time passed, the family name became gradually tarnished. There was one gay member, a couple of high-profile divorces, and one painful permanent departure of a family member into the Australian wilderness. But the climax that jolted the family was the unbelievable, spine-tingling horror occurred in 1987 when my genteel grandmother, raised in the lap of luxury with the proverbial silver spoon in her mouth, suffered a dagger pierced brutally through her heart while her mentally ill daughter slept soundly by her side, and her favorite son, an upper-class executive, inebriated from some late-night carousing, slept in the room next to her, undisturbed. We were now a scandalous, scurrilous family drowning in moral degradation.

How could I restore the family name with a literal skeleton in the family cupboard? I puzzled over the thorny question till, by coin-

1

cidence, I came across Bernard Shaw's novel but wise observation: "If you cannot get rid of the family skeleton, you may as well make it dance."

This book is the enactment of that dance. I have attempted to embed the heinous crime in so much history, both personal and cultural, with so much tradition, with so many anecdotes that the skeleton is lifted from blood and gore into an instructive story of profound irony: lives swirl and change direction unexpectedly that the wealthy are not immune from the play of this Greek tragedy and that unspeakable and calamitous events occur beyond reckoning. Fate is never fair. In truth, it has a cruel sense of humor.

In the process, I crack open the history of my ancestors, highlighting their involvement in the mutiny of 1857, chronicling their rise from outright poverty to riches and land, culminating in the CIE medal of honor bequeathed to my great-great-grandfather at the coronation of Queen Victoria as empress of India in 1877. That the beloved daughter of this illustrious gentleman would be murdered by the hand of an intruder in her son's house is an unfathomable mystery.

I have borrowed the technique of Akutagawa's psychological thriller, *Rashomon*, to explore the complexities of human nature, as family members describe their version of the murder in self-serving, contradictory statements. Each character is locked in his or her subjective perception because each character safeguards his or her ideal self by diplomacy or outright lying.

I include the talking voice of my dead grandmother who further exposes the hypocrisy and the complacency of members of the family. The ghost castigates them for dismissing her intuitions as senile fantasy and delusion. She declares them guilty of all the things they could have done that they didn't do, of all the safeguards they could have put in place but failed to. She exposes the underbelly of their psyche. "A lie," the ghost declares, "has many faces, but the truth is one."

CHAPTER 1

Om Sweet Home

It's a funny thing comin' home.
—Scott Fitzgerald

It was October of 1987. I had returned to New Delhi after an absence of seventeen years in the US. My mother's circumstances had changed drastically after my father's death in 1972. There was no car and no uniformed guard. The taxi driver pushed the gate open with a clang and parked the car at the side of the house. This was the house my mother had designed painstakingly and had built over some years. The construction workers had harassed her beyond endurance, the architect had extorted money, and any labor employed had bullied her out of her mind. A widowed woman in India is the victim of anybody she employs because there is no man to protect her. She once told me that a stuffed dead man stuck in a chair would be sufficient to keep employees from bullying a woman. A dead man commanded greater respect than a live woman. This was the tragedy of a patriarchal society. Despite the odds, a house was standing. The lower floor had been rented and my mother occupied the upper, unfinished floor. She had achieved the impossible: completed the construction of a double-story house, rented out a floor, and kept her sanity. She had a roof over her head and a rental income.

I was out of place in the New Delhi suburb. My form-fitting white shorts, high-heeled sandals, plunging neckline, and short styled hair was suitable for a shopping mall in the US. A bunch of urchins with dark eyes and shining white teeth collected at the gate to stare at the odd spectacle of a woman with long, exposed legs standing confused at the bottom of the stairway. Some unwashed faces peered from over the wall to get a glimpse of the circus queen.

I started climbing the stairs, lugging a suitcase with both hands. The stairs were unfinished and almost vertical, slathered over with a thick coat of white paint. The urchins looked fascinated by my unsteady attempts to haul my suitcase over what looked like a vertical ladder. A domestic servant peeped from a window but pursed his lips, as though he had been ordered not to speak to anyone.

This was not the India I remembered. In the past, guards, orderlies, and peons would have vied with each other to carry my suitcase and salute me enthusiastically. The fragrance of jasmine and marigolds would have suffused the air. My mother's smiling face would have welcomed me and ushered me into the prayer room to fold my hands and thank God for my safe arrival. She would have affixed an auspicious mark of red powder on my forehead. But those days were no more. My father's unexpected death had left my mother with a small pension. All niceties had to be dispensed with.

Predictably, my mother's form appeared at the head of the stairs. I hadn't seen her for seventeen years and expected to see a bowed woman with a head of gray. Instead, she looked statuesque, erect, formidable, and still a force to be reckoned with. She was a cross between the Greek goddess Athena and the Hindu goddess *Durga*.

"Take your time, these stairs are treacherous. *Dhire, dhire* (slowly). I have dinner ready for you. *Kaise thee* (how was your) flight?" She shot a volley of questions, interspersing Hindi words into her somewhat Victorian English.

We were all hybrids of Hindu/English culture with a smattering of Arabic/Persian words, the legacy of Islamic rule. I heaved to the top of the stairs. There was no warm embrace. We were not a touchy, feely family. We took pride in our austerity. Tears of joy at reunion or tears of sorrow and pain were a rarity. My mother faced the death of my father dry-eyed. I endured injections at the age of five without a whimper. She tousled my hair affectionately and guided me to the corner of a room. Here was displayed all the color and pageantry of what missionaries called "pagan India." *Durga,* the goddess of war, sat in a bloodred sari astride a tiger, her raised arms gripping the ammunition of war with two benevolent items: the lotus and the conch, and *Saraswati,* the goddess of learning, curved in unison with a swan strummed her *sitar* (musical instrument). The wall behind was plastered with photographs of her *guru* (spiritual mentor), Chinmayanand, and with portraits of saints and mystics. The altar was cluttered with powders and flowers. I folded my hands and bowed my head, requesting endurance to sustain my mother's well-intentioned but fierce disposition.

I stepped onto her spacious patio. The sides were lined with large, empty, dented, somewhat rusted aluminum canisters that had once overflowed with different grains and *ghee* (clarified butter), but which now were packed with dirt and sprouted all manner of flowers. There were thorny stalks of "kiss me quicks," long sprays of bougainvillea, petunias, nasturtiums, tufts of grass, and other nondescript shoots of weeds that gave the patio an atmosphere of happy chaos. Neatness, order, and exactness were not my mother's virtues. She excelled in artistry, creativity, and a colorful carelessness. There was a swinging bench-like contraption along the front of the patio, flanked by smaller rounded canisters crowded together and bristling in clumps of night blooming jasmine and the holy basil plant.

The upper floor was incomplete, largely brick and mortar. I could tell that the occupant had run out of money and simply made do with what she could afford.

We rocked on the swing and exchanged details of our difficult lives. Mine in the US, mostly exhausted from preparing lectures and correcting papers, attending academic conferences, paying endless bills, and trying to keep a clean, if not an orderly, house. I was a single mother which required constant attention on the physical and mental health of my children. I was raising them in a generally benevolent but mostly racist country. My children were peanut colored, the only Brown faces in a White school. This for my son was a calamity.

5

My mother's challenges were even more severe and culture specific. She had to adjust to chores that she had taken for granted in the past, such as standing in queue to get a jug filled with milk, hauling canisters on a jumpy scooter *rickshaw* (motorized three-wheeled auto), arguing, and haggling *ad nauseum* about the cost of potatoes and cauliflower. She had also lost friends to unexpected deaths and accidents. Friends had fallen away with her widowhood. Her children were in foreign countries. Moreover, activities such as banking, paying bills, and investments that were downright medieval in India were also cause for a headache. Just surviving from one day to the next was a challenge. Her only solace, she said, was her writing. She was turning out stories and novels, using her experiences as a widow in a male-dominated world as material.

"How is *Naniji* (grandmother)? I bet she's happy to be living with her son and some miles from her daughter."

There was a long, uncomfortable pause.

"My brother should have left her in Lucknow (name of a town) with my sister. She had lived with her daughter for a decade, had old, trusted friends, and felt secure. She's now in her mideighties, in a new city, and has no friends. She didn't want to leave, but my brother, your uncle, wanted to play the hero and move his mother to his house. Ironically, he's outside the house most of the day, and when he's in the house, he drinks. He's not much company."

Any talk of liquor disturbed my mother. My uncle's drinking was a big embarrassment. She attributed the habit to a Western education and the years he served in the army.

"Army life is rough," she explained, "and they do this kind of thing with liquor and women. Nobody in our family drinks or 'does the other thing' with women."

There was disgust on her face. Looseness of character and sexual licentiousness was abhorrent to her. Before reading the newspaper, she would tear out from the left corner of the *Times of India* any photograph or depiction of a woman exposing and thrusting her ample bosom and deep cleavage to the public or of a woman in a state of undress. Her standard of decency was grace and good taste, not unnecessary exposure.

I knew better than to add to her rancor or to criticize her brother. She felt she had the right to pass judgment on members of her family, but if anybody else criticized her family, she would chew them alive.

"It's 'that woman,' the *Panjabin* (woman from the state of Punjab) that has driven him to drink."

Her prejudice of *Panjabis* was deep-rooted.

"Their women are brazen and aggressive, bold and vulgar, always stuffing their mouths with greasy food. Look what they have done to Delhi. It used to be a city of grace and style. Now people stand around licking *pattals of chat* (small plates made of dry leaves used for eating snacks along streets). Their language is vulgar and loud, and they behave as though they're God's gift to the world. They've infested Delhi with their *chikni* (smooth and sleek) skins and white faces, all painted over with garish makeup. It's one of the curses of the partition of India. They've destroyed this city with their vulgarity."

"How does *Naniji* react to her son's drinking?"

"She thinks it's a form of relief from all the tension he has to endure through the day. He's under pressure. His ex-wife, the *Panjabin*, lives in an annex on the roof. Her room has a different entrance, but when your uncle is away, she comes down to aggravate your grandmother. The drinking doesn't bother your grandmother, the *Panjabin* does. She wishes his marriage had not been such a resounding failure."

I reflected on my mother's stereotypes for Punjabis: bold, vulgar, pushy, loud, greedy. I reflected that with some tweaking and change of context; they could all be positive attributes: vigorous, high-spirited, forthright. In truth, their women were refreshing in their self-confidence, and the men demonstrated outstanding inventiveness and entrepreneurial vigor. But I knew better than to argue. Moreover, I was hungry and arguing with my mother was not the best medicine to maintain my appetite or hers. I reflected that in the circumstances, silence would be the best policy. With the shades of night approaching, we moved from the open-air patio to the covered veranda. At the entrance, my mother had inscribed the sacred syllable "Om" with her unique artistry to welcome me. The syllable was outlined with flour, instead of chalk, with a double line made of golden turmeric and deep-red chili powder. Tiny marigolds covered the empty space with one deep-red one accenting the crest of the syllable. Her ingenuity made me smile. A line of entrepreneurial ants were already feasting on the flour. I sidestepped to avoid smudging her artwork and squashing the ants.

Despite my mother's acerbity, the experience was still "Om Sweet Home."

CHAPTER 2

Visiting My Grandmother

I was now in an unfinished room that served as the dining room. The walls had not been painted, and there was a roof that kept the rain out and the house dry; but otherwise the upstairs looked like a lower-middle-class dwelling. This was somewhat anachronistic because the house was located in a gated community. The title of this elitist neighborhood translated as "Greater Heaven No. 1." In a short time, we would travel to "Greater Heaven No. 2," which unbelievably would be the location of my grandmother's murder. The old woman's heart would be pierced with a dagger while she slept, hardly a heavenly act.

My mother was defensive about her unfinished dwelling. "The downstairs has a marble chipped floor and pale-lemon-colored walls. It's grand!" she said with pride in her voice at her accomplishment. "*Bahout bariya* (very fine). It's rented to a decent man, a *shareef* (honorable) man, but his Bengali wife is…" Her voice trailed off.

Mai kya battou (What can I say)?

"Don't talk to anyone on your way out," she admonished. "We're not on speaking terms. *Bilkul chup* (totally silent). *Sar me dard kar diya hai* (given me a headache) *us aurat nae* (that woman)."

Later, I would hear about the neighbors on either side and the litigation that was in progress. I concluded that there was much turbulence in Greater Heaven No. 1. But I was also confident that my mother with her fierce energy and fearless demeanor would win the case. She knew how to handle scoundrels.

While she was laying out the table for my especially prepared dinner, the phone rang.

"Don't pick it up!" she shouted impatiently from the kitchen. "Your grandmother phones *roaz* (every day) about faces appearing and *gayab* (disappearing). *Mai tang ah gai* (I'm sick and aggravated) with her *kahaniya* (stories)."

I was puzzled and disturbed by my mother's indifference which bordered on callousness. Out of respect for my grandmother, I picked up the receiver.

"Sheela, Sheela, *kaha ho? Kaha ho?* (Where are you?)" It was my grandmother's trembling voice.

"*Mai* Dolly *hoo* (I'm Dolly)," I said, using the name she knew me by.

"*Acha, tum aa gai* (So you're here)," she responded, still tense with fear.

My mother yanked the phone from my hand and spoke impatiently to her mother, telling her to control herself. She accused her of being senile and of imagining horrors. She reminded her that she was in her son's house and that nothing could touch her. I could hear my grandmother's terrified voice denying that she was imagining things, that the strange face at the window sent a chill down her spine, that she had nobody to speak with except Vimla, a daughter who had lost her sanity in her teens.

"*Suno, suno* (Listen, listen)."

I couldn't stand the terror in her voice and her helplessness. I yanked the phone out of my mother's hand and consoled my grandmother with "*Mai aa rahi hoo* (I'm coming). Aa*k dam aa rahi hoo* (I'm coming immediately)."

Leaving my dinner untouched, I ran down the flight of stairs onto the highway to find transportation. After a frantic search, I hailed a pedicab. My mother had now joined me and had changed her mind. She agreed to accompany me to console and support her mother, though she was convinced that all the apparitions that terrified her were in her own mind. She believed my grandmother had read too many horror stories and was projecting her fears. She continued her litany of complaints and rationalizations. My uncle's house was about three miles away. As the pedicab driver pedaled along the highway, my mother lamented on my exhausting flight, my empty stomach, the debacle of a dinner left on the table, the delusions and hallucinations of the senile, the ill timing of her mother's call, and the foolishness of her mother who left a secure and warm place in Lucknow to settle with a son, who was always out of the house. By the time we reached our destination, her litany of complaints had turned into a whine. She felt that her mother had turned my arrival, a time of celebration, into a dirge. We walked through the ostentatious wrought iron gates designed with rococo swirls to the marble-floored entrance and knocked at the door.

My grandmother peered out, leaving the chain intact, reluctant to open till she was sure it was my mother. Her mentally handicapped daughter, crudely labeled "Mad Vimla," followed. The girl was like a lamb following her shepherd. She could not be separated from her mother.

She greeted me warmly, stroked my hair, and thanked me for coming so promptly. She was dressed in a cotton, green-checked housecoat. I had only seen her wearing silk in the past. Cotton was beneath her. She apologized for her appearance and labeled her cotton housecoat as *raddi* (cheap trash). She continued to caress my face and hair while making a humming sound as though assessing my character.

"*Jab chti thee tum chalti nahi the, bhakti thee* (When you were young, you didn't walk, you ran)."

My mother commented that, as an adult, I continued to run, that I ran marathons and actually ran around the world.

My grandmother's second comment was that I did the right thing in leaving my husband and going to the US.

"*Vo acha adami nahi tha* (He was not a good man)."

The comment made my mother explode. She castigated her mother for being totally traditional when it came to her own daughter's marital decisions but so modern and downright liberal when it came to her granddaughter's life.

My grandmother remained unfazed. "*Vo samay doosra tha, ab doora hai* (Those times were different, we now live in different times)."

The two kept sparring about my grandmother's double standards while I looked around the room. The most conspicuous item was a display of arms on the wall that was opposite the stairway that the ex-wife would use secretly when her ex-husband was out of the house. The grandiose display consisted of a shield, four lances, two daggers, two rifles, and other smaller ornamental military ammunition. Each item was highly embossed with what looked like a design that incorporated three metals: brass, copper, and steel. Had the items been polished, they would have lighted up the wall, but they looked neglected and dull.

My mother explained that the entire display on the wall had been a gift from the king of Nepal to her brother in appreciation of services he had rendered to the Nepalese king. The ammunition had been awarded to him in an elaborate ceremony. On the opposite wall, there were black-and-white photographs of a tall, stalwart adventurer wearing headgear and dark glasses. He cut a fine figure of a man with his tousled hair, deep, dark eyes, and rugged good looks.

Had my uncle really been such a handsome hunk? I wondered.

His features looked chiseled with a "Misra" nose and a strong square jaw. The "Misra" nose characterized all the members of my grandmother's family, including myself. Curiously, the Misra family came in all colors, from dark ebony to milk white, but each member was characterized by a straight, narrow nose that ended in a slight bulge, slightly to one side, and therefore asymmetrical. His hair was thick, black, and tousled. His complexion was dark and glossy. He radiated vitality and good health. I noticed his erect posture, his broad chest, and his flat stomach.

The uncle I knew before I left India was mostly balding with patches of white and blotches of dyed hair, mostly unkempt. His coloring had an ashen cast. The stomach was loose and protruded conspicuously, falling over as though draped over his trousers. He walked like someone who was in an authoritative position and knew how to throw his weight around. The belly flapped and jiggled as he walked.

His pajama strings were untied and dangled untidily over his protruding stomach. From small talk about memories of my childhood, the conversation moved to what would constitute a horror story. It was unnatural because one associates gray-haired grandmothers with fulfilled senility, a mature kindness, and for what one associates with the golden years of a life well lived. But what I was about to hear was closer to a grisly soap opera.

I noticed that there was a dagger missing from the symmetrically arranged display on the wall. My mother noticed the blank spot also and explained that my grandmother was paranoid about the dagger on the right side. She would hoist herself on the sofa, remove it, and hide it behind the heavy cushions of the seating arrangement in the living room.

"Why?" I asked in puzzlement.

"*Dar lagta hai* (I have fears)." She followed this statement with a shudder and moved her eyes in a surreptitious manner to face the stairway.

"She thinks," my mother explained, "that she will be murdered by that dagger. She's obsessed with the idea. Every day she removes it, and every day my brother returns from work and installs it on the wall."

My grandmother could understand and read English, but she couldn't speak it. She now addressed my mother, "*Brahm nahi hai. Sab sahi hai. Ye aurat muje jinda nahi rah Ne de ge. Nahi zinda rahne de ge* (I am not deluded. Everything is true. This woman will not let me live. She will not let me live)."

"How will she benefit by killing you?" I questioned. Then repeated the question in Hindi.

My grandmother moved from her chair to my sofa and positioned herself, so I could hear her clearly. Deafness ran in the family. She wanted to be certain that I would understand the underlying motivation of the ex-wife.

"*Sona hai, purane zamane ka. Makaan hai. Property hai, will hai. Sab mere nam hai* (There's gold, of the old kind, there's a house, there's property. It's all in my name)."

My mother continued where my grandmother left off. She explained that my uncle had had three heart attacks. He was afraid he may pass away before his mother, so he had willed everything to her.

"The ex-wife thinks that your grandmother will bequeath nothing to her. Thus your grandmother's death would take care of the dilemma. If your grandmother was out of the way, his three daughters would inherit his property which would give the ex-wife the opportunity to avail herself of his possessions. *Vo bari tez hai. Sab samaj liya hai. Judge ki larki hai, will ke bare me smajti ha* (She's very sharp. She's figured out everything. She's the daughter of a judge and understands the importance of a will)."

My grandmother followed my mother's reasoning and added, "*Mai uske raste me hu. Agar vo mere jan le, to property uske ho jay gee* (I'm in her way. If she can take my life, all the property will be hers)."

The information was disconcerting. I did not think my grandmother was paranoid or the victim of senility. I walked to her bedroom to identify the window where faces appeared and disappeared. My nostrils were assailed by the smell of urine. It was so strong that I staggered backward. Vimla, the mentally ill daughter, was lying in bed unaware that she had urinated.

I returned to the living room to report the strong stench of urine in my grandmother's bedroom. Something needed to be done.

I could have spoken to the wall. My words fell on deaf ears. Apparently, the stench was a permanent feature of the room, and there were more important issues to attend to. My grandmother was reporting the disturbing activities of the ex-wife. She would come down the stairs, fix her gaze at the dagger, then fix her gaze at my grandmother, and go back and forth as if to suggest that the dagger would be used on her person.

I asked my mother why my uncle allowed his estranged wife to reside in his house. Their divorce had not been friendly, and the acrimony had increased with time. Her interpretation of events was that the ex-wife had occupied an independent house in a shabby neighborhood. She had expressed fear for the safety of their college-going daughter who would be followed and whistled at by the local *goondas* (unruly ruffians). She complained that the atmosphere was not suitable for a young woman, and she feared for her daughter's safety.

My uncle swallowed the story and had his ex-wife move to the *barsati* (roof) of the house with their daughter. The studio apartment had one independent stairway on the outside and one that gave access to the living room that was supposed to be out of bounds for her, but which she used in defiance of his orders when he was away from the house. My mother added that his ex-wife was seeking entry back into the house and that this was the first step.

I asked my grandmother: "*Kaise tabiyat hai aab?* (How are you feeling now?)"

She smiled. "*Aab kutch shanti mille* (I have some peace now)."

She walked us to her bedroom window. Our noses were again assailed by the smell of urine. My mother held her nose. Vimla, who had been waiting for her mother, sat up. She appeared oblivious to the smell. The window was directly opposite the door. It was dark outside, and nothing was visible.

Vimla behaved as though she didn't follow the conversation. She remained in a half-reclining position, braiding and unbraiding her hair. My mother insisted that it was grandmother's imagination and that she was projecting her fears into dark places.

"She always had an active imagination. Her letters to me read like a novel."

"D'you think she's imagining a gothic tale to amuse and frighten the daylights out of herself?" I asked, hoping that my mother was accurate in her conjecture.

"Yes, she tends to exaggerate. In years past, Lucknow was once flooded. Instead of cars, there were boats floating around her house. She looked down from her upper-story house and painted such a vivid picture of the flood and the fear of her drowning that your father and I took a train to Lucknow. The flood had receded, and things were normal. *Bilkul pagalpana* (total madness)."

My mother reminded my grandmother of the past situation where she had created such panic for no reason.

"*Nai, nai! Ye farak hai. Ye sahi hai. Mere jan ko katra hai* (No, no, this is different. This is real. My life is in danger)."

Vimla may have followed the final sentence. She appeared to understand that her mother's life was in danger. She got up, walked to the side of her mother, and put her head on her shoulder. Her sari was soiled, her face was distraught, but she had sufficient empathy to sense her mother's fear. We changed the sheets hurriedly and sprayed the room with a mosquito repellent since there was nothing else available. My grandmother took charge of her daughter's soiled clothes. Vimla now followed us back to the living room.

My grandmother sat next to me. She extracted a crumpled Rs.100 bill from her housecoat pocket, ironed it out on her knee, looked at me with pleading eyes, and said, "*Dolly, jab mai mar jau, tum Vimla ke bare me puchti rahna* (Dolly, when I'm dead, keep asking about Vimla's welfare.)"

She gave me the note. The moment was poignant. I sensed her hopelessness and her helplessness. Her daughter, my mother, would not believe her predicament, so she was going to rely on her granddaughter who lived in the US. She followed this with an apology for not having given me time to rest after such a long *suffar* (passage).

After assuring my grandmother that I would come again whenever she wanted me and bidding her a deep *namaste* (folding hands in salutation), I tried to convey my goodwill to Vimla by putting my arms around her. My mother said her farewell with less sentiment. She reminded her mother that she was living in her son's house, that he was a very important person, and that no stranger could enter the house, leave alone remove a dagger from the wall and stab her. She made the entire event sound absurd to the point of being downright comical.

We returned home in an auto *rickshaw.* It had been a long day with unexpected convolutions. I took to my bed without dinner but tossed restlessly. I had the troubling feeling that my grandmother was not imagining the face at the window. It was not a delusion of a senile mind and that her plea for protection needed to be addressed by her guardian, my uncle.

CHAPTER 3

Memorable Ancestors

I had barely opened my eyes when I heard my mother's voice, "You don't need to be confused, you're in your mother's house in New Delhi. You arrived yesterday."

It was a perfect orientation of my whereabouts.

"There's a bucket of hot weather for your *gusal* (bath). After your bath, we'll have breakfast. I've made your favorite *aloo ke paranthe* (flat bread stuffed with potatoes) with *dahi* (curd). At around ten o'clock, a young, sprightly girl will come to wash your clothes, scrub the dishes, and water the plants. She's a real character, very outspoken, well-informed of all the gossip of the neighborhood, and a master of abusive, vulgar language that she hurls at the domestic staff on the first floor. I'm teaching her to read and write Hindi. With her around, you won't miss the absence of a TV. Her name is Sundari (beauty)."

The bathroom was almost primitive. There was a low stool made of wood to sit on called *pathri;* a large steel bucket with a silver finish with steaming hot water; a second bucket for cold water; two mugs, one for pouring water over myself and the second for the toilet. There was no toilet paper in any Indian house. There was also a bar of soap and two towels made of cloth which had no traditional toweling. These were called *angocha*. The traditional way was to wash the towel after the bath on a daily basis and put it out to dry. The *pathri* (low stool) allowed for a scrubbing of the feet with a red-colored pumice stone called *jhava*. The Indian way of bathing was efficient. One bucket of hot water sufficed for one person.

I came out refreshed and eager to taste my mother's cooking. This is not to say that she enjoyed cooking; she complained that it came in the way of writing her stories. She often cooked with a sheaf of papers on a clipboard under her arm, ready to resume her endless scribbling with the dozens of pens I bought for her from the US. She was one of those rare mothers who appreciated the gift of a functional pen more deeply than a gift of a gold bracelet. But despite her dislike of cooking, stuffed flatbread was one of her specialties, and she did succeed in making fine pickles and containers of smooth curd.

After breakfast, my mother disclosed her program for the day.

"I will not live forever," she said with an expression of resignation. "Death is our most reliable friend. You can depend on him to escort us to another world."

I wondered what manner of homily was about to follow. Would it be a reading of John Donne's *Death Be Not Proud* or Emily Dickinson's quaint lyric on death courting her because she failed to court death? My mother was well acquainted with Western literature with a special fondness for George Eliot, Bernard Shaw, and Virginia Woolf. She was also a closet feminist castigating men for subjugating women when in truth they couldn't equal the female sex.

She was also athletic, an unusual passion for an Indian woman. When I asked her what attribute she had missed in my father, she replied promptly that he didn't play tennis.

The statement made sense in the light of what I learned about the family. Her grandfather, Heth Ram, had set up the Hindu Tennis Club in Bareilly with eight tennis courts in his properties. He played tennis till he died at the age of eighty-four. One of his sons was the tennis champion of India. After my mother introduced me to the modern spirit that was reflected in her grandfather, I understood her love of athletics and her passion as a writer. She looked at chores such as cooking and cleaning as beneath her dignity. It took time away from more worthwhile endeavors.

All this I learned when she handed me a pen and a notebook with the command, "I'm going to narrate the history of my family

starting with your great-great-grandfather. The dates may be somewhat inaccurate, but the history of the family and its accomplishments are factual."

She felt that once I understood the massive, unimaginable
prosperity my grandmother had lived with and inherited—she was
bequeathed four villages, countless gold coins in steel containers, and
a massive treasure of jewelry, brocades, silks, and satins as her marriage dowry—I would understand her obsession with wills, gold, and
property and her fear of somebody dispossessing her or her son to
whom she had bequeathed valuable property. She was behaving like
a responsible caretaker of her father's earnings. She was a hen sitting
on her eggs. She was the golden goose who was being targeted for
death in her old age.

We were now interrupted by our domestic help, Sundari. She
entered with a jolt and erupted into a furious condemnation of the
staff downstairs. She complained in her shrill fourteen-year voice that
they did not treat her with respect. The house, she asserted boldly,
was of *her* employer. They were only renters, so why were they putting on airs.

She greeted me with a *namaste* (Indian form of greeting) and
asked me to teach her English, so she could impress the snobs on the
bottom floor. Wait till they hear where you're from! She stuck her
head up as though that would be her trump card.

Sundari was skinny and as jumpy as a live wire. She lurched as
she walked. After she had washed the clothes, cleaned the kitchen,
and swept the floor, my mother, always an educator, would give her a
half an hour class in the Hindi language. She carried a shabby satchel
with a notebook. With me in the house, she was planning to capital-
ize on her good luck and add English to her curriculum.

We now settled on the much used stuffy sofa to hear my mother
recount the tale of my ancestors. From time to time, Sundari would
sing a tune from a Bollywood movie, drop the broom, and enact
a hip-shaking dance movement, swinging her hips seductively that
would make us smile. She was very much a Bollywood fan. After her
laughter subsided, my mother got to work in earnest.

"I'll start with your great-great-grandfather. His birth is not recorded but he died in 1828, so we can assume that he was born in the late eighteenth century. His name was Pandit Gulab Singh (Gulab means rose). But he was no pandit and violated all *Brahman* caste taboos, eating meat openly with great relish."

From what had been reported to my mother by my grandmother and from what she had gleaned from family gossip, Gulab Singh had had a senior commanding position in the police service. He was in command of the police station at Bareilly, a town in the northern province. He was considered a man of importance, and according to his son, my grandmother's father, who was sixteen at the time and already married with one child, his father cut a grand figure in his uniform and his shining brass helmet.

My mother reported that he had a large, sturdy build and excelled in wrestling. It was a rare man who could down him. He lost his wife early in life and replaced her with a mistress, who was rumored to have been a dancing woman in the past. At the time, when women were in *purdah* (behind curtains), it was a common practice to cohabit with a woman for outdoor life and recreation. It was considered part of the genteel breeding of an educated "modern" man. Sunder Singh trusted this woman and gave her complete control of his finances.

When he passed away unexpectedly in 1828, his mistress appeared to mourn him deeply and lamented his demise with loud cries of anguish. Secretly, however, she got hold of all his assets—gold, cash, and whatever—and disappeared from the town, leaving the young son, Het Ram, destitute and with no means of survival.

With the disappearance of the heartless gold digger, Het Ram looked for work. His knowledge of Persian did not help him because with the coming of the British, all work was transacted in English. He was told by well-wishers that he should seek admission to a British school. The school was awarding scholarships to all students who aspired to learn English. The general populace was reluctant to learn English for three reasons. The first: the schools had a covert policy of converting students to Christianity. In addition, there were caste taboos that forbade *Brahmans* from entering into interaction with *mlechas* (foreigners who were seen as unclean). The second: it was one more ploy to extend imperialist policies to subjugate the masses. This attitude finally culminated in the bloody mutiny against the British in 1857.

The third reason was colorful, even though irrational. My mother smiled and tittered when she described how Indians were flabbergasted by the physiognomy of British faces, especially the teeth. The teeth looked larger than life, were prominent on the face, and with the strong jaw bones that characterized their faces made them look like horses. The women, especially, were described as horselike. This puzzling feature was attributed to the movement of the jaw when speaking English. The rumor was that if you joined the school and learned English, you would look like a horse.

I burst into laughter. It was ironic that while the British characterized Indians as feeble, womanlike, and Ganga Din's (a metaphor derived from Rudyard Kipling's poem), the Indians had their own pejorative images.

My mother paused here and arranged her notes for the new epoch in Het Ram's life.

In the meantime, Sundari served us glasses of *shikanji* (Indian-style lemonade) with sprigs of fresh mint leaves held in place with two ice cubes. She informed me that she was interested in learning choice abuses in English that with their venom would dumbfound her enemies on the bottom floor. Her body was as skinny as a broom handle, and she was in the habit of striking a pose with her left hip vaulting to one side and her right hand on her hip.

I suggested that she would get further in life with words of reconciliation. "Why do you want to play the battle axe? Ignore them."

"No," she retorted with the earthy common sense that characterizes the labor class. "You have to fight fire with fire." She added that her mother had a foul mouth and added an Indian version of the cliche, "The apple doesn't fall far from the tree."

I looked up at the bluish sky and the scudding clouds turning an angry gray-blue. The sky was overcast, and at any time, the porch would be drenched with sheets of water. An outpouring of rain in India often felt like a heavy torrential shower that washed all the dust-laden trees that lined the roads into a fresh green. It was time to retreat indoors. The covered porch would be thrashed unmercifully, and my mother's flowerpots would overflow with splashing streams of water and falling, liquid dirt.

We moved indoors. I reclined on the bed; the upper half of my body supported by a bolster and some pillows. My notebook was on my lap. My mother sat in an easy chair with her untidy sheaf of papers. She was never without some kind of a manuscript. I can recall how when close to death in 2011, at the age of ninety-three, she lay on a low sedan, turned on her side slowly and painfully, and after rummaging through some artwork on the floor, selected a cover for her final publication. Her agent, seated on the ground, waited patiently, and in some amazement at her presence of mind and her total attention to the project. She died a week later.

"Where were we?" she said, speaking to herself.

"The English school," I reminded her.

"I'll complete this section, and we'll have lunch. If it doesn't rain, you must visit the Lotus Temple. It's fabulous."

The narrative continued to the sound of Sundari's pitter-patter and the clink of china in preparation for lunch. I learned that Het Ram was admitted to the school readily. He was offered a scholarship of four *annas*, the equivalent of less than four pennies. Pathetic as that sounds, for the mid-nineteenth century, four *annas* was substantial. His food and other necessities were covered by donations and supplies from people who had known his father, Gulab Singh, as a police officer and a wrestler. As time passed, his wife sold her gold bangles and finally her more expensive utensils. Het Ram's first challenge was to learn English and pass the examination. In order to accomplish this, he had to overcome his stammer. He did this by cramming his mouth with pebbles, in the manner of Demosthenes, and then attempting to pronounce the English alphabet. After years of practice that required enormous persistence and willpower, he achieved his objective. He only stammered when he lost his temper, but for the rest, no speech impediment was detectable.

His second challenge was to stay awake late at night and to literally burn the midnight oil in order to pass his examinations. Kerosene had not been discovered; his source of illumination was a *chirag*. This consisted of a clay container filled with mustard oil with a cotton wick immersed in the oil and arranged to hang out of the container. The wick was ignited with a matchstick. If the flame ebbed, mustard oil was added. The sixteen-year-old Het Ram pursued his English studies by the meager light of a *chirag*.

In order to arrest sleep, he tied his hair with a cord and affixed the cord firmly and tightly to a rafter or hook on the ceiling. Any nod of the head tugged on his hair, which in turn pulled at his scalp. The pain would make him sit up instantly. This strategy to banish sleep was not the boy's invention; it was practiced by earnest students generally at the time.

My mother left to give the final touches to the lunch. Sundari had cut the vegetables, but my mother did the cooking. We would continue dialoguing over lunch. It was best not to break the thread of Het Ram's biography.

No spoons or forks were needed for lunch. The fingers would suffice. Had we lived in a village, no plates, chairs, or even a table would be necessary. A large green plantain leaf would serve as the plate; I would have sat cross-legged on the floor, and the plantain leaf would be placed on a freshly washed and dried floor. And the bowls? They, too, were made of dried leaves that had been stapled together with fine slivers of wood, similar to toothpicks. No washing of dishes or harsh detergents were required. The plantain leaves would be used as fodder for goats and cows, and the cooking vessels would be scrubbed with ashes from the wood stove. The traditional Indian way of cooking was eco-friendly, but modern civilization condemned such eco-friendly habits as backward.

I observed that India was scientific in its day-to-day habits of living but that science as a subject was developed in the West. If the two civilizations synthesized their wisdom, it would be a resounding win-win situation.

My mother's response was that I should wash my hands because there would be no steel between my fingers and the food. She added that she would recount anecdotes and incidents she had heard in the family circle. She was five years old when her grandfather expired.

Her memories of him were faint, but gossip about him was in the air; and one of her mother's favorite topics of conversation was the extraordinary life of her father.

So I broke a portion of flatbread, shaped it like a spoon, scooped up a portion of okra, and felt I was in heaven as the spices titillated my tongue. I think it was Dennis Prager, the popular American show host, who declared that in his view, Indian cooking was the best of all the world cuisines he had tasted and that if he lived in India, he could easily be a vegetarian.

His words never sounded truer. What impeccable judgment!

CHAPTER 4

Het Ram's Accomplishments

"Around 1876 or it could be 1879, my grandfather was placed in charge of settlement work in Rewah," my mother recounted, trying to get the dates as accurate as her memory allowed. "My notes will have the exact date. You can check."

The rest of the remarkable incident went as follows: He made the acquaintance of the *Maharajah* of Rewa (King of Rewa), who was an ardent *shikari* (hunter) and had shot as many as a hundred tigers. The walls of the palace had frescoes depicting memorable incidents in which his courage was highlighted. He was a tall, muscular man. The guns he used were extremely heavy and were loaded with silver bullets of ten tolas each (117 grams). The guns were so heavy that only one *sirdar* (officer) could raise it to the shoulder for shooting. But the Maharajah could walk miles with the gun on his shoulder. My mother's narration was staggered and slow because she was trying to masticate at the same time. I have smoothed it out to make it coherent.

On *Dashera* (festival that shows the victory of good over evil), he and his brother, also a tall, muscular man, would dress in heavy armor and shining breastplate and enter the compound on caparisoned elephants to the sound of drums to add color to the pageantry of the festival.

The Maharajah suffered an accidental death, and my grandfather along with the British District Magistrate had to settle accounts and divide the property among his four or five wives. There was a strong rumor, supported by the wives, that a secret cellar in the basement area housed an enormous amount of gold and cash.

"A British colonel was given the job of exploring every cellar and every corner of the palace, but he recovered nothing. The job was assigned to your grandfather. He went with a band of stalwarts at night with torches and made a thorough exploration from one end of the palace to the other. Lady luck was with him. Late at night in a dark corner of one of the cellars, the band found several large boxes full of rupees worth an incalculable amount. The boxes were loaded on carts and taken under proper escort to the bungalow of the political agent."

The colonel, whose name my mother was unsure of, possibly a man named "Berkeley," was much impressed by the integrity of Het Ram. He was aware that my grandfather could have diverted some boxes, and nobody would have been the wiser. His integrity and scrupulous devotion to duty earned him a reward and a promotion.

I was ready for dessert, but my mother's recount of the anecdote had slowed her down.

"I'll save the other stories for later," she said.

There's a road named after him—Het Ram Road. People talked about how things were before Het Ram and after Het Ram. He was the dividing line between a corrupt past and an efficient present. It was like the dividing line between DC and AD. But all these honors were conferred later.

"What I'm trying to get across," said my mother, "is that your grandmother was raised in the lap of luxury. She only wore silks and, even as a young girl, had a collection of tasteful jewelry. She even had a British nanny who taught her to read and write English and the finer British customs of entertaining, laying the dining table, shaking hands, knitting, embroidery, and crochet. Two maids trailed her when she walked, fanning her to keep mosquitoes and flies away from her damask skin. That this pampered lady is now in her old age teetering on a couch, lifting a dagger, and concealing it under cushions, that she is lying next to a mentally disabled daughter, that her son is frequently drunk is unbelievable."

"That she enacts this bizarre drama because she fears being murdered rocks the imagination," I added.

"That's all in her imagination," my mother insisted, she's hallucinating.

"And perception is reality, but what if it's not perception but the actual reality. What then?" I questioned.

Just then the phone rang. It was my grandmother. She expressed great happiness in seeing me after more than twenty years and requested me to stop by on the weekend after I was well rested.

"*Bhoolna mat* (Don't forget). *Mujhe kntch bat kahni hai* (I have something to tell you)."

My mother wrested the phone from my hand and reprimanded her mother for putting stress on me. "*Abhi, abhi to aaye hai, use* relax *karne do* (She has just arrived. Allow her to relax)."

"*Koi jaldi nahi,*" my grandmother responded, "*Kisi bhi din aa jaay*(There's no hurry. She can come any time)."

Sundari, in the meantime, requested some English abuse words.

"May all the flies of India and Africa settle in your belly button," I exclaimed, recalling inaccurately a farcical comment by Dick Cavett.

"*Ya, bahoot lamba hai. Chota vala* (This is too long. Give me a short one)."

"Knock it off?"

"*Naak eet aaf.*"

"It means *chup kar* (shut up)."

She repeated it as though saying a rosary, "*Naak eet aaf, naak eet aff.*"

I was puzzled by my mother's reluctance to give ear to my grandmother's fears. She just refused to dwell on or resolve the situation. The easiest solution would be to send my grandmother back to Lucknow into the loving embrace of her daughter and grandson from where she had been removed. She would be back in contact with friends she had cultivated over a lifetime. Ironically, she paid nothing for board and lodging in Lucknow, but she insisted on paying Rs.300 a month to maintain her dignity in the New Delhi home. After the horrific event of her murder, we would recognize the supreme irony: She was forcibly taken by her son to the theater of her murder and supported herself, despite her palpable fears and foreboding, by paying her prosperous son a stipend of Rs.300, which he was not allowed to reject. She even had an uncanny intuition of the instrument that would be used for her slaughter. She knew where it was hung and did her best to conceal it to save her life. Death courted her. She did not court death.

I recalled how in the past, my mother had been much more empathic of grandmother's anxieties. She had been instrumental in finding suitable husbands for her sisters and had transported her father to our house for the best treatment for his kidneys. Why had she changed? Was it that her struggle to maintain herself with a modicum of decency in a country that treated women as second-class citizens had eroded her emotional reserves? In the recent past, her effort to survive had been a heroic struggle. She would literally hyperventilate and lift her face toward heaven in describing the day-to-day harassment she had endured in trying to negotiate with construction workers and contractors. It was literally widow-baiting. The objective of the contractor was to break her will, kill her slowly, so she would fall on her knees and be reduced to a living corpse for the consumption of his insatiable appetite.

At this painful juncture in her life, my daughter was in my mother's custody. She was bold, self-assured, and spirited despite her three years. Some days later, my mother gave me the following comical but moving account of the child's *hutzpah*. She smiled in remembrance of an instance when a contractor was attacking my mother with ugly words and choice abuses. The three-year-old was not going to put up with this gross abuse of her grandmother. She found the stoutest stick that she could handle, positioned herself behind the bully, and with her total three-year-old prowess, she whacked him on his buttocks.

The man turned around with irritation and reprimanded her, "*Kya kar rahi hai larki?* (What are you doing, you damn girl?)"

My daughter retreated, pretending she was playing innocently, but as soon as the bully turned his back, she smacked him with three swift whacks—*thack, thack, thack*. After the contractor left the patio, rubbing his rear end, she positioned her stick in a convenient spot for further action if he returned. She was hell-bent on giving him a thrashing. My mother was so helpless that her only supporter at the time was a three-year-old who did not suffer bullies gladly. She also put a smile on a suffering widow's face.

My painful divorce, the insecure future of my children, my father's meager pension, the excruciating stress of building a house had all accumulated to such a pitch that her nerves had been eroded, and she simply pushed away or averted her head from any further responsibilities, especially when they appeared unrealistic or unimaginable. After all, her own emotional survival was at stake. I was reminded of the wise cliché, "If you're not for yourself, then for whom? And if not now, then when?"

There is one additional factor that pleads for a voice. On my last visit to my grandmother's house, just one day earlier, she had disclosed with much satisfaction that she had been president of the Lady's Club in Lucknow. When she first joined, there were only five members. When she retired, the clientele had increased to one thousand. Club activities were part of the heritage of her illustrious family. Het Ram had established a tennis club, and two of his sons were global presidents of the Rotary and the Lion's Club.

Her assertive disposition and creative faculties as well as her social life had preserved her zest for life. The sudden and unexpected transplantation from a small town that honored her social contribution to a busy metropolis, where she was anonymous, shattered her sense of self. She was confined to the company of her mentally challenged daughter and a son who frequently drank and smoked heavily to anesthetize his fractured emotions. He had already suffered three heart attacks, and the litigation involved in his divorce had been bitter and extended. His life had been scrambled.

He heard his mother but did not listen to her. What she wanted was an empathetic ear. She wanted a listening ear and an understanding heart. My mother likewise was impatient. She talked over her, reducing her mother's nervous, fearful words to a heap of dead leaves, the inevitable rotten harvest of a senile mind not worth listening to.

Gradually, she would retreat into herself, her words an unheard wail in an alien, heartless, urban establishment.

CHAPTER 5

The Glory of the Ancestors Continued

Every man is a quotation from all his ancestors.
—Emerson

My mother was telling me about my roots. I realized that the roots are more important than the easily growing branches of a tree. The tree could only achieve the height that the roots determined. In a manner of speaking, our ancestors lived in our blood. We were simply a continuation of our ancestors in a visceral way. For example, just as a person of fifty is related to his earlier self of thirty, in the same way, an infant is connected with earlier ancestors. The child does not emerge from a blank space but from a space teeming with ancestors. These ancestors live like ghosts within the child. The child will also be an ancestor in time. In reality, history begins before we are born.

I remember a Korean girl in my class who described that Korean ritual required the memory of ancestor names going back eons. In all, she had to recite some seven hundred names. It was considered bad luck to forget a single name. To forget was to break the link in a connection going back into the past. This quaint tradition, along with ancestor worship, now made more sense. Not to know your ancestors is to deprive yourself of a treasure house of memories that could restore life. It's to be a tree without roots. I now listened to my mother more intently, and I might add more gratefully. Her recollections felt like man-making or human-making.

I was inspired to learn that my great-great-grandfather employed untouchables in his service, choosing to break with orthodox tradition. One of them, named Cheta, a *chamar* (untouchable) by caste, was a family favorite. He was put in charge of family arrangements and the care of the children. At one time in the near past, his touch would have been pollution and extended ablutions and rituals would have to be performed as a cleansing; but in the Het Ram household, he was the valued heart of the household. If any of the children disrespected a gardener's child or the washerman's daughter, they were made to apologize, not just in words but by compensating the humiliated child with a gift of two annas from their pocket money.

The dignity of labor was instilled in the children. Het Ram did not depend on servant help for his everyday needs. He made his own bed, rearranged furniture by physically lifting chairs on his own, dusted and cleaned his room, arranged his clothes, and transacted his chores without servant aid. The adoption of this mode broke with convention and shocked visitors.

Although he valued Western science and Western values, he preserved those Hindu traditions that he felt were beneficial. For example, he remained a vegetarian, eschewed smoking and liquor, abhorred all stimulants, took daily walks, and generally avoided all habits that he believed would lead to moral degradation. He also made an effort to reform his bad habits: irrational obstinacy and a rotten temper. In his final days, he wrote hymns to Krishna that have been preserved and passed on over the years. They are written in Hindi, have literary merit, and reflect his personal devotion to the deity. He did not convert to Christianity but was admiring of the ethical principles he learned from the gospels.

These were some general thoughts that my mother had heard in the household. She was only five when he died, but she did have some faint memories of riding with him in a *Landau*, the posh coach of its time, with a uniformed orderly standing on the outside. She remembered the sights, such as snake charmers, folk dancers, and the like, along the road.

"I have told you some things from the top of my head," she said, arranging her notes with unfaded black-and-white pictures of a gallery of family members who had passed away. "My grandfather's major contribution was in the mutiny of 1857 and the greatest honors bestowed on him was the Companion of the Indian Empire medal (CIE) at the Durbar to celebrate the coronation of Queen Victoria as Empress of India in 1877."

Apparently, this was a topic much discussed in the family, and she needed to refresh her mind of its historical background. My mother was a writer and was reluctant to pass on information carelessly. For example, when referring to the coach brand "*Landau*," she strained to recall the exact name, refusing to settle for Phaeton and other brand names.

"No, No," she exclaimed, "I rode a L...La..." She furrowed her brow till the correct word popped in her mind.

Once she had the word, she was able to recall the exact details of the uniform of the guard that stood on the steps of the Landau when she rode with her grandfather.

While flitting through her sheaf of papers, she came across a list of subjects that my grandfather studied for matriculation. The formidable list of subjects made me feel illiterate. In 1855, the highest examination had the following curriculum: Arithmetic, Algebra, Plane and Spherical Trigonometry, paley, bacon, essays in English and in Urdu, translation from English to Urdu and *vice versa*. A boy was expected to pass each subject in one year. The class book in English literature contained biographies and criticisms of all great English writers, several plays of Shakespeare and of other dramatists.

Het Ram passed all the subjects while struggling with poverty and maintaining his wife and child. He was zealous, almost to a fault and became a great favorite of the principal, Mr. V. Tregear, but unfortunately, the principal died before Het Ram had completed his studies. The principal was deeply mourned. Het Ram visited Tregear's grave frequently during his lifetime.

We took a break. Sundari served me my tea in a stainless-steel glass with a question on her face.

"Why do you drink tea in a stainless-steel glass? All *maems* (ladies) use fine *paslain* (porcelain). I feel *sharminda* (ashamed) of using a glass, but I won't tell anyone."

I had to smile at her honest disclosure. Domestic servants learn the more sophisticated manners from their employers, but I was reverting to *desi* (local) ways, even though I lived in the US and was "foreign returned." She also complained that my abusive expression, "*naak eet aff*," did not have a sting in it. The servants downstairs laughed at her with "*Naak kya?*" (*Naak* what?). Clearly, I was a failure in her eyes.

She then whispered something secret in my ears, "*Mujhe iska ho gaya* (I'm in love). *Mai batau* (should I tell you?)."

At the time, I had no idea that this minor flirtation would metamorphose into a major catastrophe of unrequited love that would impact her young heart in an almost fatal way.

The tea revived my mother. She was ready to roll. Her mental energy astonished me. I requested her to change the subject from her grandfather to his daughter. I was sated with my great-grandfather's lofty accomplishments. He had outperformed himself. I now wanted to hear about his daughter, my grandmother. The elite in India is more often than not light-skinned. It was puzzling to me that my grandmother, the daughter of one of the richest men in Bareilly, was married to a Ram Gopal Misra, who was in the Provincial UP Civil Service. He was tall, statuesque, very impressive, highly educated, but still a dark-complexioned man who professed to be a theosophist. True, he was a friend of Annie Besant and through her of Bernard Shaw, but still, his dark color was out of place in their household and their circle of friends. I had learned through experience that in India, color was destiny. Skin-lightening products were as profuse as suntan lotions in the US. Even housemaids with their meager salaries invested in *gora karne ka* products (skin lightening).

While rummaging through my mother's black and white photographs, I came across a photo of a team of Englishmen, who looked like cricket players, standing in three rows for what looked like a group photograph. I asked my mother what they called themselves as a team. My mother chuckled at my absurd assumption and explained that they were neither British nor cricketers; they were her uncles, mother's brothers, in tennis-playing garb.

"They could have fooled me!" I exclaimed.

There was not one iota of difference. They looked British through and through.

"But why is it that the members of your mother's family are either milk white or chocolate? Why did they arrange the marriage of their exquisite daughter to a dark-skinned man?"

"That's a story in itself. I was planning to narrate it to you. Now's a good time."

The story goes that the exquisite daughter of Het Ram was slated to marry a light-complexioned Brahman man from a prosperous, highly reputed, established family.

The date of the marriage had been fixed and the invitations sent to literally thousands of people. One fateful day, a domestic female masseuse, who went from house to house to give massages, requested an appointment with Het Ram. She disclosed that she had sensitive information to communicate.

What she disclosed is that the prospective husband of my grandmother had a skin disease that had left white patches on his upper thighs and back. She was sure that the family had not disclosed the malady to anyone but that it would be advisable that a doctor check out the condition prior to the formal marriage. She also intimated that the prospective groom would avoid the medical examination.

In negotiating arranged marriages, it was customary to secretly question domestic servants about the habits of the family and the disposition of the prospective bride. In my grandmother's case, the information was volunteered. It was customary for marriage parties to conceal any negative information, such as prior operations or allergies, that would weaken the prospect of a marital commitment. I had heard of brides married without the groom knowing that she had only one lung. I also knew of men who negotiated marriages in prosperous families by keeping their one-kidney status secret. There were other deceptions: dark-skinned women were powdered to look white and introduced in dim light to create the illusion of a fair skin. Sometimes the deceptions were bolder: Light-skinned women were employed to impersonate the prospective bride. In most cases, neither the fake woman nor the daughter was aware of the deception. After the marriage, they had to face the music and the consequences. The situation would trigger family feuds that lasted for generations.

Het Ram was a health faddist. His selection of food was wholesome. He was also highly conscientious of his children's health, readily summoning a doctor at the faintest symptom of ill health. The masseuse's disclosure disturbed him deeply. He took immediate action. Putting together a team of doctors and skin specialists, he hurried to the house of the prospective bride to demand a medical examination of his body.

The news traveled fast through the town and reached the ears of the family of the prospective groom. A band of medical experts descending on the groom was unwelcome to their family. They felt their *izzat* (honor) was at stake and that norms of decency had been violated.

In my mother's words, "The groom had left the house in a*palki* (sedan) in a state of nervousness. He was about a mile from his house when he spotted the medical team. Afraid of being cornered and undressed, he jumped out of the sedan that was being carried on the shoulders of four men and disappeared into the *khet* (pastureland). The weeds must have been tall because he could not be found. He had made his escape and had confirmed the suspicions of Het Ram that he was dealing in damaged goods. Why else had he jumped out of the sedan and bolted into the pasture?

"The marriage to the light-skinned groom was cancelled, but since the invitations had been issued, the event could not be called off. There was only one option: The groom had to be replaced and replaced in a hurry. Mr. Ram Gopal Misra, my grandfather, was the new choice. In truth, he was an extraordinary man, very tall, strongly built, scrupulously honest, a writer, and amateur actor with a well-paying job in the Civil Service. His only shortcoming was his deep pigment, even though his coloring was radiant."

Het Ram, who was scientific by disposition and education, was above color prejudice.

"A man's character," he declared, "is not shown through his pigment. It is the result of geography and climate. It is one millimeter deep. It offers no clue of the character that lies beneath."

Further, Het Ram was not going to allow a sliver of epidermis to cancel the opportunity of having this talented young man as his son-in-law. So the bond was sealed. The date of the marriage remained the same, though the groom had been replaced with a better but darker man.

My grandmother reported that there was shock among the wedding guests. They looked at each other with raised eyebrows and questioned, *"Kala kaise?* (Why Black?)" The word "*kala*" reverberated and was in everyone's mouth. "*Kala, kala, kala, kala, kala,*" wagged their tongues. It was unbelievable that the exquisite, White princess was being wed to a Black prince. Nobody had told them that a man's character is determined by the content of character, not the color of skin. Nobody had told them that constellations of dark-skinned ancestors were glowing and downright radiant in that skin. Their conditioning of color prejudice was so deep that it made them blind to those attributes that matter in a human being: a good heart and a sound character.

And how did my grandmother react to the switch in prospective husbands from White to Black?

"In those days, girls did not know who they were marrying. The 'suitor' would be given the opportunity to see them at a visit to a garden or a concert or shopping or at the house."

"So girls had no choice?" I asked.

"Fathers were aware of their daughter's tastes and kept them in mind. Your grandmother more than loved her husband. She adored him. She was a happily married woman. Her woes commenced after she had children."

CHAPTER 6

Beginnings of a Fractured Marriage

Divorce is the psychological equivalent of a triple coronary bypass
—Mary Kay Blakely

My mother disappeared into the kitchen. Sundari was cleaning the utensils so vigorously that the upstairs was resounding with the banging. Was she making war with the kitchenware? We were going to have *khichri* for dinner. This was one of my favorites as a child. It was a concoction of potatoes, cauliflower, peas, carrots, and onions mixed with long-grained rice and cooked with plenty of water, a spoonful of salt, and a couple of spoonsful of turmeric, which had been ground in the house in an iron pestle. After the rice was boiled and the water evaporated, the grains would take on a beautiful saffron color. The yogurt was homemade, and the cilantro paste had been ground between two heavy slabs of stone called a *silbatta.* This old-fashioned method of crushing herbs released the flavor much more strongly than the whirling blades of a blender.

My mouth was watering. I would add a large spoonful of hot, sizzling *ghee* (clarified butter) to my portion. *Khichri* was served on a stainless-steel *thali* (plate) with a small salad of cucumber, tomatoes and green chilies, yogurt sprinkled with red chili powder, and salt, and the *dhania chutney* (cilantro sauce). Eating out on the patio surrounded by a chaos of green and burgundy foliage was like old times.

Skinny Sundari with her two plaits hanging to the sides, her bright, defiant eyes, and saucy mouth was our chef.

But there was still time before I could enjoy my supper. I still had to hear the dramatic story of the glamorous, voluptuous, outspoken, rebellious *Punjabin* (from the state of Punjab) who threw a monkey wrench on the complacency of the family.

My mother was always reluctant to address the subject. It was difficult for her to accept her brother's weaknesses and even more difficult to address her own culpability as observed by outsiders. For the most part, she considered herself a victim of the gossip perpetrated by the estranged wife in trying to avoid her own responsibility in her wretched marriage.

I once overheard my mother complaining to her beloved brother, "Do you know how my reputation has suffered in trying to protect your interests? Have you any idea how our family name has been compromised?" She made these accusations in a crumbly, complaining voice that was tired out by the unexpected turns and twists in his inharmonious marriage.

To even mention her frustration to her beloved brother demonstrated the depth of her fatigue. She was losing her voice on the subject and would massage her throat upward when trying to establish her innocence.

His final divorce was possibly the most peaceful event in the total warfare. After the divorce, the intimate skirmishes moved from close range attacks to volleys of verbal missiles fired from a distance, and the release of venomous gossip that poisoned the atmosphere.

"Where did your brother meet his future wife?" I shot the first question, trying to establish a chronology of the emotions and how they frayed and became defunct.

"Your father and I introduced her to him," she said, turning her eyes upward at the heavy and explicit irony.

"How did that happen? Did she make a great impression on you?" I was squirming in my chair at the thought.

"Your grandmother wanted us to arrange her son's wedding," she said. Then she followed it up with the narrative: "My parents did what was done in most *Brahman* families. They consulted an astrologer about the suitable season, auspicious dates, and so forth. The astrologer's response alarmed them. 'Your brother,' the turbaned astrologer said to my mother somberly, 'is going to fall into the clutches of an evil woman who will destroy his family, wreck his health, and finally destroy his life. She will have a *chikney* (smooth and sleek), white, creamy skin, black snakelike eyes, raven-black hair, and a heart made of flint. He will be in her clutches for decades.' He compared her with the *vishkanyas* (poison damsels) in ancient India who were fed snake poison over a period of time to kill enemies, such as Alexander the Great, with a lethal kiss."

Needless to say, my parents left in agitation. They were aware that my uncle had served in the army and had relinquished the taboos on sexual conduct, such as sexual abstinence before marriage. They feared that he would acquire a girlfriend or some modern-day dancing woman who would wreck his life. He needed to be protected by being safely joined in wedlock to a woman from a good family. Their intentions were good. They attempted to preempt the event but, in the process, fulfilled the forecast. The event was Sophoclean in irony. My uncle was a modern-day Indian Oedipus.

"What then?" I exclaimed in suspense. "What happened next?"

"In our search for a suitable bride, we ran into a very refined lady who was married to an IFS officer. They were three sisters in all. She suggested that we consider her sister.

"She arranged the meeting. My father found the girl highly desirable in beauty but not particularly refined. He sensed that she was somewhat aggressive and took exception to how aggressively she served herself food and with what masculine gusto she chewed it. He attributed these traits of excessive vigor to her Punjabi ethnicity. As an ethnic group, they were known for their assertiveness in business, their bravery in war, and their gusto for living. Their women tended to be bold and robust. They were capable of beating up their husbands if circumstances called for it. The tradition of women from Uttar Pradesh (one of the states in India) conformed to the Victorian idea of submissiveness and femininity. They were the ones who threw themselves on the funeral pyre of their husbands."

My mother's estimate was mostly negative. What passed for beauty in *Punjabis* was their creamy-white skin. In her view, beauty was in the refinement of features, the arch of the brow, the softness of the eyes, and, above all, the expression of gentleness in the face. A woman was considered beautiful when she had a calming and ennobling effect on whoever she interacted with. She also had reservations about her table manners. My mother's sentiments were not new to me. I had read a slim pamphlet on how a woman's character could be foretold by the way she chewed her food. This preoccupation was not limited to India. I had also come across a Victorian essay on how to choose a woman by observing her eating habits. It appeared that this Punjabi woman's eating habits did not fit the bill of refinement as accepted in India and England. But the family was in a hurry. My parents concluded that it is not they who were marrying this girl but my mother's brother. It was his final decision. If she was acceptable to him, why should they object? She was undoubtedly good-looking, tall, statuesque, but not actually slim, a kind of rotund voluptuousness, and, above all, creamy-white, the hallmark of beauty in a pigment-obsessed India.

My uncle was duly impressed by her beauty and enjoyed her assertiveness.

"They were a modern couple. Submissiveness, devotion, service, caring, patience, modesty had all been thrown out the window. She was the stuff you could fly around the world with, enjoy cigarettes and liquor with, play bridge with, have sex and enjoy porn with. And so they tied the knot that took many decades to untie and climaxed in the bloody murder of my mother."

"What happened next?" I questioned, wanting my mother to unpack the next chapter in the growing horrific drama.

"After the marriage," my mother continued, "it was customary for the bride to touch the feet of all the elderly family members as a sign of respect."

I was aware of this custom. When the bride bowed to touch their feet, the elder members of the family lifted the bride up tenderly and blessed her.

From my mother's account, this modern bride acted differently: "After touching a few feet, she retorted, 'How many do I have to touch? How many times do I have to bow?' She made it sound like an unnecessary chore, an archaic tradition that could be dispensed with."

The faces of the women turned pale; the men's faces fell. These were grand figures who had sacrificed for the family. We, the younger generation, sat on their shoulders. Such contempt was unthinkable. But they swallowed the insult and concealed their humiliation. The marriage had to go on.

The honeymoon eroded the trust between them. There was some finagling with money, some extravagant spending, some mutual attacks on family members, door slamming, and other inharmonious bickering. My uncle started calling our home; my parents supported him psychologically and emotionally. His wife called her siblings and friends, and the poison spread.

My mother, always the protector of her younger brother, advised him vociferously and frequently. His wife objected to her chronic interference. He continued to lean on her, making short visits to the house. He was drinking and smoking excessively and had no peace of mind, although he was flourishing professionally in his high elitist positions.

The ill will increased. There were accusations of adultery, of untruthfulness, of unreliability. This scenario was punctuated by the birth of three children in all, all girls. It was both comical and unhinging to see how closely the pregnancies followed door bangings, separations, and accusations. Both hoped for a male child, a necessity in a patriarchal culture, but the yen remained unfulfilled.

Somewhere along the line of endless battle, litigation was introduced. There was talk of separation, alimony, child support, and other bounty that follows mutiny. My mother continued to feud in partnership with her brother.

"Mummy, this is a sensitive subject," I hazarded in a diffident voice. "But she holds you responsible for the disharmony in her marriage. Do you regret the role you played?"

"*Bhai, bhai…bhai* (a colloquial, linguistic mannerism that allows a person to pause). He was my younger brother. It was my duty to protect him. When your grandmother gave him birth, I stumbled like a sleepwalker into the operating room. I was three years old at the time and was carried out promptly. There was a reason I appeared on the scene. I have always played the role of protecting him. I was his shield. Should I allow his wife to make a fool of him? If she is flirting with her husband's boss and he has evidence, should I stay silent?"

She then related how when the divorce was in process, she had a visitor—the ex-husband of the youngest of the three daughters. His divorce had been a nightmare. The charges were of a sexual nature, but the true nature of what had occurred was not clear.

He came to warn my mother: "I want to warn you about these sisters. I'm not exaggerating when I label them 'monsters' and 'bitches.' They will stop at nothing. I have been married to one of them, and I'm acquainted with their sinister ways. Listen to me! Wash your hands clean of them. I sleep with a bodyguard to protect me and four killer dogs, each tied to one *paire* (post) of my bed. Yes, four killer dogs, and I still don't feel safe. They will stop at nothing, nothing."

This was damaging testimony that provoked a memory of my own that had unnerved me. I was married into a high-profile family in 1966. At the reception in New Delhi, the then prime minister of India, Lal Bahadur Shastri, and other dignitaries were invited to celebrate the union. I was standing about ten feet from the seated figure of Shastri. People were surrounding me in a loose circle, but there was no congestion. I was accessible to any guest who wished to greet me.

Suddenly, the estranged wife of my uncle broke the circle and moved toward me. Personally, I held no grudge against her. On the contrary, I was always admiring of her beauty and her free lifestyle.

"I have something for you," she said, moving close to me and casting a surreptitious sidelong glance at anybody who might observe her. "Open your hand," she said, and repeated, "Open your palm. I have something to give you."

Being the unsuspecting innocent that I was, I opened my palm. She pretended to place a ring in it, but actually simply rubbed the ring on my palm with some pressure; and instead of giving me the ring, grasped it with her fingers with a quick movement and disappeared out of the circle with a smile on her face.

I was nonplussed. Why did she pretend to give me the ring? I wondered. When I mentioned the incident to some relatives, I saw fear in their eyes.

"*Are beta usne to jadu tona kar diya* (Oh, my child, she has done black magic)."

This is how they explained *jadu tona*. It's the use of supernatural powers for evil and selfish purposes. It is the malicious left-hand path, the counterpart of the benevolent white magic. By pressing the ring in the palm of my hand, she was stealing my vital essence or vibrations and paying a *tantric* (sorcerer) to invoke lower spirits to blast my marriage.

Confided in a common friend that she was going to destroy my life to teach my mother a lesson. What lesson? The trials and tribulations of a woman who is abandoned by her husband and must run from pillar to post in order to survive with a modicum of dignity. Dinner was on the table, and Sundari was chomping at the bit. She wanted to wash the dishes and retire for the day.

I smiled at the irony of the situation and the unexpected twist of fate. She may have given my already potholed marriage a final sorcerer's lethal blow, the ultimate karate chop. What it did was to release me from an oppressive marriage. It gave me wings. I could now fly to the US and earn a PhD. Bravo! I'm in total agreement with Oscar Wilde, "Divorces are made in heaven." And I might add, "Some marriages are made in hell."

Coincidentally, she met me after my divorce and commented in astonishment, "But you're so happy. It's the happiest I have seen you."

I spooned the saffron-colored *khichri* reflectively into my mouth. My divorce was cause for celebration. Even my father commemorated the moment with the declaration, "Hang the bastard!"

"Sometimes you get the best light from a burning bridge." This thought-provoking observation by Don Henley was true of my life.

I owe her one. I had stepped into the greatest version of myself by her nefarious arts.

CHAPTER 7

Vimla's Insanity and the Curse of Dark Pigmentation

*She was a prism through which sadness could
be divided into its infinite spectrum.*
—Jonathan Safran Foer

It was now the fifth day. I felt soaked in family history, but there was still one mystery that remained to be unraveled: Vimla's insanity. I was aware that she was not born with a mental problem. There were photographs of her as a schoolgirl and as an adolescent. She looked no different from the girls around her. I also knew that the members of the household avoided addressing the subject. They talked around it. On one of my early visits, I felt she was a ghostly presence, an invisible entity that appeared and disappeared unnoticed. I could hear her walking back and forth on the roof. Her footsteps had a distinct rhythm as though she was being propelled by a force that she could not control. Was she walking to keep herself from thinking?

When I questioned my mother, she teared up. Although Vimla's mind was opaque, she was able to pick up on clues: a new sari, cosmetics, sandals, and other details of attire that suggested something was afoot. She did not resist but actually cooperated with the sensitive process of being presented to the suitor.

Vimla was tall, slim, and charming, but she had inherited her father's dark complexion, which did not go in her favor. All the foundation and powder could not camouflage the dark pigment below. There was another factor going against her: Her younger sister was a classical beauty. She resembled a popular actress and was often teased by men, "Hello, Meena Kumari! Hello! Hello! Meena Kumari!" On occasion, people gathered around her for photographs and signatures, thinking she was *the* actress. It was common knowledge in the town that the first, my mother, and the fourth one were the beauties in the family. The others were dark-complexioned. This deep-rooted, irrational prejudice contributed to her mental breakdown. "Black is beautiful" was light-years away. Whiteness had so blinded that generation and, in truth, this one that they were blind to the radiance of the darker complexion. It was a status symbol to be seen with a white-skinned woman.

As events would turn out, three men in succession refused her after meeting her. In the India of the time, this was termed "rejection." It was considered a humiliation that only a very hardheaded woman could endure with equanimity. The average woman would hide her face in shame. The loss in esteem was so devastating that most parents made sure that their daughters were not even aware that they were being "looked over" by a prospective suitor. It could have been prevented, but now it's too late.

"As you know, we were five sisters. It was imperative that each of us find a husband, but the responsibility of the selection and marriage was not ours, it was strictly the responsibility of our parents. In fact, to have a 'love marriage,' the common term for carrying out a secret love affair and refusing all other suitors for one's personal choice, was an overbold step and a risky move that would jeopardize the prospects of all other female members in the family. It was commonly understood that only girls who had no one to arrange their marriage used this option. They were considered 'cheap.' A marriage was an alliance between families. In a manner of speaking, it was families that were betrothed, not individuals. When families became estranged, the marriage often fell apart."

Of the five sisters, Vimla was the third one. She was an earnest student. In fact, her teachers described her as gifted. When our father wanted to change her school, she protested and pleaded that she be allowed to remain in the school. She was attached to her friends and was respected by the teachers. Still, her father, for reasons we don't know, changed her school. She sulked, ate fitfully, stopped communicating with people, and went into a low-grade depression. Her favorite place to hide herself was the roof of the house.

Her behavior was not taken seriously. It was dismissed as adolescent rebelliousness. She was acting obstinate because she did not get her way. While in the throes of this depression, further disappointment, quite unexpected, struck.

My grandfather was in the process of arranging a marriage for her. She was kept in the dark about the proceedings. Thus she would never learn of the rejection. But in this case, there was a carelessness in handling the situation and a dismissal of the girl's emotions. This second blow after the change in schools wrecked her mind.

She isolated herself, refused to join the family, turned hostile but never violent. At the event of the marriage of the younger sister, she beat her chest with her fist repeatedly, muttering angrily: "*Mere shaadi* (My marriage), *mere shaddi* (my marriage), *mere shaddi* (my marriage)." She felt she had been replaced by her younger sister, and the injustice rankled in her breast. She was removed from the marriage grounds and bundled out. She retreated to the roof, continuing her cry of "*mere shaadi* (my marriage)."

What followed was even more tragic. The event exposes the inhumanity of Indian society. It was, to invent an adage, the last straw on the camel's back. The charade would leave her permanently damaged.

Some simpleminded women suggested that the unmarried girl had sustained an emotional shock and should be married without too much emphasis on the status of the family and other niceties of the marriage process. Acquiring a husband would give her the satisfaction of marital fulfillment.

The policy turned out to be disastrous. Vimla was too far gone. Her heart broken repeatedly had mended itself with scar tissue, scabs had formed to stop the bleeding. It was like parchment that had been ripped over and over again and could not be healed. She still beat her chest but had forgotten the spasmodic, shrill cries of injustice. She had forgotten the source of her pain.

At the marriage ceremony, her menstrual cycle stained her wedding sari. She was none the wiser in observing the blood stain on the silk petticoat and her ankles. There was horror on the faces of the sisters. They bundled her up in shawls and carried her out. The ceremony was interrupted by the gross pollution, but the merriment, the false grinning faces, the prayers all continued. She was brought back in a fresh sari and seated by her husband. He peered through his curtain of marigolds and jasmine to make sure all was well.

I sat transfixed listening to the unbelievable horror. Was it her heart bleeding? Did the blood seep through the scar tissue and the scabs? Was it her heart telling her that her desire for marriage had been fulfilled, but the drizzle of sacred water would have to be blood? Had a knife suddenly slashed through her heart and loosened an artery?

The next day, she was packed in a car with one sister by her side to make sure that she did not break out in a howl of pain or jump out of the car. Marigold and jasmine garlands rose like a swelling orange river to her chin. Her mother believed that the warm embrace of her husband and his kisses would restore her sanity.

What actually occurred was almost comical if it had not been so tragic. Even my mother covered her face so that she could hide her smile. I burst out laughing and could not contain my giggles. They came in spurts and just about suffocated me.

The drama went something like this: the groom tried to exercise his conjugal rights. Vimla, who had been taught early in life to safeguard her virginity, raised herself and gave him a tight slap across his face. If the slap did not stun the groom, the subsequent thrashing he endured catapulted him out of the bed. He landed with a thud on the ground. The blows continued to rain on his head. She protected her virginity. Her hymen remained intact. She had shielded Indian womanhood bravely.

"Who witnessed this? Actually nobody. This was reported to me by my brother. The groom, a professor of mathematics, had not included this situation in the equation. 'I thought a woman would make my life more comfortable—some good food, some pleasure… But what I received was a thrashing.'"

Vimla was returned to her home and continued pacing on the roof for the greater part of the day.

After some months of taking her to mental health clinics, the doctors recommended electric shock therapy. According to my mother, the therapy worked beyond the expectations of the family. Vimla spoke coherently and appeared to respond to life normally. However, the family did not fulfill the one essential condition that the doctor had recommended for her recovery: She had to be removed from her earlier environment for an extended period of time to give her mind relief from the oppressive memories of the past.

She returned home much earlier than the recommended period. Slowly, her mind succumbed to depression and finally regressed to its original incoherent blabberings. She never recovered. Her one consolation was her mother. She followed her around, ate with her, and slept at her side.

"Your grandmother was infinitely patient with her. Some of the time, she could not control her bladder, but this was not a constant feature."

My mother paused and added reflectively, "When there are so many children in a household, parents naturally pay attention to the healthy ones. The marginalized fall through the cracks."

Sudari served us tea with fritters and chutney. I could tell she lived in her own Bollywood world of song, dance, passion, clandestine love affairs, and high drama. She had such a strong life force that I didn't think any setback would wreck her life. The way things unfolded, my assumption would be tested in the following year.

Dark pigment had been a strong factor in my aunt's tragedy. But this raised a question: Why was it that Sarla, some years younger than my mother, who had also inherited her father's radiant black skin, had married successfully and from everything I knew of her life was very happy. She was not only dark but also stout. How had she acquired a husband?

The question made my mother smile in a surreptitious way as though there was something not quite right about the transaction.

"It was a misunderstanding."

"How so?"

"Her mother-in-law thought I was going to be her daughter-in-law. She was in a state of shock."

The story went like this: Nobody had been told that a prospective future mother-in-law would be coming to see Sarla, my mother's younger sister. She was told to dress up for a late afternoon trip to the cinema. My mother was visiting her family at the time and also freshened up to accompany Sarla to the movies. They were both seated in the living room. My mother was knitting a sweater, and Sarla was paging through a magazine.

A lady walked in and was introduced to both the sisters. They greeted her and made nothing of the visit. Both were fixated on the idea of the movie later in the afternoon. The lady engaged my mother in a conversation about her studies, her love of the sitar, her passion for tennis, and so on. She then turned to Sarla and they both chatted about Sarla's lessons in vocal music, cooking, and other pastimes. Both the girls exchanged glances furtively. They feared that if this woman stayed too long, they would be late for the movies.

After exchanging some more pleasantries, mostly addressed to my mother, the lady departed to their father's office, and the two sisters left for the movies. When they returned, Sarla was embraced by her mother who had a smile on her face. She whispered in Sarla's ears, "*Rishta tai ho gaya* (You have been betrothed)." Sarla beamed with pride, and my mother teased her fondly by pinching her cheeks.

On the day of the wedding, the bride's mother looked seriously unsettled. She had assumed that my mother was the bride she had selected. But it was too late, and nothing could be done. My mother was already married and was just visiting her parents. So Sarla was married to a veterinarian, a tall, strongly built man.

"Was the groom taken aback?" I asked, almost hyperventilating at the unbelievably surreal events in my mother's family that had never been disclosed before.

"No, he hadn't seen either of us and was depending on his mother's choice."

"Did he object to her dark color and humiliate her?" I asked nervously, fearing the worst for my favorite aunt.

"No, Sarla was one of a kind. She could tell a tale with such enthusiasm that her listener would have been left spellbound. She also had a sense of humor and kept people laughing. She was nonintellectual, full of life, kept the house alive with song and dance, and liked nothing better than to dress up in all her finery in the latest fashion. She considered me a big bore with all my intellectual pursuits. Her husband enjoyed her outgoing nature. She had succeeded in transforming the fiasco of her marriage into a work of art. She was living proof of the adage: Character is destiny."

While my mother was narrating the latest installment of her family's dramatic history, I remembered an incident that had occurred when I was around fourteen. We were going to visit an older woman. When the car neared her house, my mother expressed astonishment at the turn of events that had catapulted this woman from the lap of luxury to the shabby place in which we were about to meet her.

The two women exchanged pleasantries. My mother expressed deep admiration for the superb lawn and flower arrangements in the mansion that this now elderly, gray-haired, gout-ridden lady had occupied in the past.

"Each leaf of the house plants was polished to a shine. The silver of the vases and ornamental plates was so brightly polished, it could blind by its shine. I would be in a state of awe when I stepped on the polished floors of her house."

I could tell that the lady had a soft corner for my mother. The purpose of the visit was to thank the elderly lady for the gift of a piano that had been in her possession. She was a Christian, at a time when few Indians had converted. Her standards of cleanliness, order, landscaping, and furnishing were more European than Indian. Her possession of a piano was also a Western acquisition. Indians possessed *sitars, tablas,* and harmoniums, not pianos and guitars. As a Christian woman, she had played gospel music for church gatherings and popular lyrics for friends at bridge parties.

When my mother was ready to leave, the lady put an arm around my mother's shoulders and said in a sad, caressing voice, "Oh, Sheela, you know the misunderstanding." She had tears in her eyes.

I noticed a look of embarrassment on my mother's face that she tried to conceal by raising her forearm to her eyes.

With a half-smile, she whispered, "This is how it was meant to be."

While coming down the stairs of her upper story, rudimentary brick and mortar construction that was called a house, I said with the curiosity of a fourteen-year-old, "What was the misunderstanding? Why was the woman crying?"

"She thought I would be her daughter-in-law. I was her choice. But it was Sarla who became her daughter-in-law. There was a switch." Her voice was matter-of-fact.

She refused to answer my questions that followed. A fourteen-year-old, especially a talkative one, could not be trusted with such family secrets. But now as a mature woman with a patina of gray and crow's feet, I was now old enough to hear about the event as it had occurred. I could now connect the dots. On our way back to the house, my mother kept shaking her head in disbelief at the change in circumstances.

"She lived like a queen, now look at her! Her husband passed away, and the stepchildren threw her out of the house. She was the second wife and resented by them when they learned about their family history. In truth, they should have been grateful. They owe everything to her: education, breeding, profession…everything."

There was one more incident that proved the authenticity of the misunderstanding. Sarla and my mother were sitting on a bed and conferring sentimentally about old times. Their heads were almost touching. My mother's pale, ivory-like complexion against Sarla's darker, more passionate face. Suddenly, Sarla leaned over and clutched my sari as I walked past her into the dining room. Her face was upturned; there was deep pathos in her eyes and some gratitude.

"Dolly," she said, "if it had not been for your mother, I may never have got married. *Unhi ne mere shadi kari hai* (She is the one who got me married)." Sarla acknowledged her debt now that they were close to death. *Unke chahare se aik nahi, do shadi, ho gai* (her face achieved not one marriage but two)."

The dishes had been cleared. Sundari was nibbling at her bar of ice cream, the prize she earned for being a responsible domestic help. She was standing on the edge of the patio, leaning over to catch a glimpse of her heart throb, the uniformed driver. She had convinced her fourteen-year-old romantic heart that the driver yearned for her as she did for him. That he was shy and so pretended not to see her. No one had told her that love is blind, that Cupid was blindfolded for a reason, that love was a gamble, that there were no guarantees, that her infatuation could be a shipwreck. Her bar of ice cream was sweet, but her phantom lover, washing the car of its dust on the busy street below, was infinitely sweeter. "Did she know," the words of a wise man, "that when love gains sight, it dies."

CHAPTER 8

Final Meeting

Revenge, the sweetest morsel to the mouth that ever was cooked in hell.
—Sir Walter Scott

The next day, against my mother's protests, I hailed a bicycle *rickshaw,* handed the wiry driver the address of my uncle's house and cradling a dessert of *gulab jamun* (milky balls in rosewater, scented syrup) in my hands in a clay pot, one of my grandmother's favorite desserts. I hoisted myself into the *rickshaw.* I wanted to bid goodbye to her before my departure to the US. Somewhere deep in the dark forest of my unconscious, far from the light of day, I may have known that this would be my last visit. The way events unfolded, my next glimpse of her would be a black and white shot on the cover page of the *Times of India,* announcing the occurrence of a murder in my uncle's house.

The slow purr of the turning wheels of the bicycle brought back another memory. When my father died unexpectedly in the early seventies, I hailed a *rickshaw* from the Agra train station to the house. When I gave the name and address to the *rickshaw wala* (driver), he shook his head sadly and wiping his face with a cloth that he used as kerchief to tie around his head, he muttered, averting his eyes and shaking his head, "The commissioner is no more."

"I know," I said, surprised that even a commoner at a train station had learned about my father's death. "I'm here to see him. I'm his daughter."

On that dark day, I heard the same whirr of the bicycle wheels, rhythmic and steady, as if they said, "The wheels of *karma* (every action has an equal and opposite reaction) move slowly but surely." When the rickshaw pulled over on the gravel driveway with a looming *amaltash* (Indian laburnum) tree that I had known so well, shading it, I handed a sheaf of notes to the driver.

He refused the payment. "I cannot accept this. He was loved by the people. You have suffered enough."

I was deeply moved by the empathic response of this man. Destitute as he was, he would rather suffer the loss of the money than add a mercenary note to the burden of a mourning woman, the daughter of the deceased. It was moments like this that restored my faith in India. Empathy may have been absent in the rich but was warm and flowing in the poor.

The rickshaw purred on, past the vendors hawking their fresh fruit; past the washerman ironing a shirt with his tea is a steel glass on the hot coals; past the school children in uniform, bowed by their load of books; past the cobbler striking his anvil; past the baskets overflowing with garlands of pearly jasmine and crimson marigold; past peasants and laborers in diverse, colorful attire. There was no monotony, no uniformity.

This busy road, like millions of other roads, characterized diversity and inclusion. Each man and woman was a law unto himself and herself. Saris in colors such as deep purple and bright yellow shimmered in the sun and, despite the wandering cows, the dust, and the roadside garbage, proclaimed loudly and unabashedly the chaos and the undying vitality and vigor of an ancient civilization. An Islamic proverb popped in my mind, "A lot of different flowers make a bouquet." The scene was indeed a flying bouquet.

I was at the house, a handsome, upper-middle-class, double-story mansion with a *barsati* on the roof (a shed to protect from rain). I banged at the door; a bolt was lowered, a face peered out, a chain was released, and the door opened wide.

"Welcome, welcome. Your grandmother informed me of your arrival. So happy you could squeeze in some hours to visit." It was my uncle, his voice full of goodwill.

He was older, heavier, and slightly hunched. He reminded me of the tall, burly cops in my county who approach slowly, surely with an air of authority, their bellies hanging over their trousers, and moving slowly like a bag of meal to give a ticket after a traffic violation. There was a clear sense of executive authority in his demeanor—somebody who was used to giving orders. His hair was unkempt and streaked in shades of gray, white, and rust. The roots were white, the ends dyed black with discolored strands of rust. This mop had not seen a comb since the morning. One could tell that if some layers of fat were removed from around the jaw and chin area, his originally chiseled features would emerge, and if he lost some eighty pounds, he would present an imposing figure. But there was a sense of neglect and carelessness. Someone who had put his hands through his hair in bewilderment too often and someone who had taken recourse to liquor to numb his emotions. This was not the uncle I had known.

My grandmother approached me, dragging her right leg behind her. Vimla, her mentally challenged daughter, followed her like a lamb.

"*Kaise ho* (how are you)? *Acha hua aa gai* (I'm glad you have come). *Sab bacche door hai* (All the children are far away). *Pata nahi kab mile ge* (Don't know when we'll meet again)."

I turned my head furtively to look at the dagger. It was missing. My uncle had not replaced it. It was probably under one of the cushions. That meant that she had either encountered the sinister face of the estranged daughter-in-law or the terrifying, mysterious face at the window in her bedroom.

I presented her with the *gulab jamun.*

She smiled. "*Tumhe yaad hai mere pasand* (You remember my preference)." She held the clay pot to Vimla's nose. "*Tumhare leye hai* (It's for you)."

My uncle ordered tea and *pakoras* (vegetables fried with spices in gram batter). It was like old times. Pleasantries were exchanged. We talked about our children, all scattered in different countries, all professional, all following in the footsteps of Het Ram's commitment to Western education.

I described how my mother was acquainting me with the family history, and how her gift for writing and literary flair made the material especially engaging.

"Jolly good!" exclaimed my uncle. "My grandfather's experience in the mutiny of 1857 needs to be chronicled. I can fill you in," he said, hitching up his pants and rising to the occasion.

He described how Het Ram was part of the British office staff. His work was to read the vernacular communications and reports, to translate the relevant ones into English, and to make translations of English orders, notices, and proclamations as were issued from time to time. He marched with the British troops into Fatehpur town. He saw corpses of the rebels who had been caught and punished. He saw hangings. He described how without the Enfield rifles and the discipline of the British and Sikh troops, the Muslims may have had a better chance of restoring the Mughal empire.

"I have the historical documents with exact numbers of troops if you're interested. One of the historical documents," he declared, "describes the prayers that the Muslims recited from the Quran as they fired at the captive British soldiers. There were beheadings on both sides and betrayals."

My grandmother wanted to sing the praises of her mother, Hardevi Kumari. She described her as "a great beauty," who commanded the respect of "even important people." She was a treasurer and a money lender, not just a housewife. She followed this up with descriptions of her parties in which groups of women gathered to sing and dance. "She had a good singing voice." She described her pilgrimages to all the important temples, and her donations to religious fakirs (wandering religious mendicants) and orphanages. She continued to harp on the riches, jewels, and silks that surrounded her, on all the sedans she rode on, all the domestic servants that accompanied her, all the women that fanned her. My grandmother, her only daughter (she had numerous brothers), was pampered in the manner of a princess. She had an English nanny.

The enthusiasm in her voice and the light in her eyes clearly demonstrated her pride in the past but also an awareness of her changed circumstances. There was nostalgia in her voice but also an

57

underlying grief. She looked like a woman seeing a rainbow through a veil of tears. There was a half-smile and an unshed tear. It was a face that was afraid to smile or to cry. She knew too much to smile; her detractors knew too little to justify her tears.

She was sitting in her son's house, who was oblivious of the danger to her life. She had concealed the dagger, the instrument she feared would end her life. Her murderer, she intuited, occupied a shed on the rooftop. Her mentally ill daughter was sitting beside her with her head on her shoulder. She was her sole support. Her son who was singing the praises of her father had none of his moral integrity or his Spartan habits. He drank heavily and fell into a stupor countless times. Some considered him an alcoholic. His life was hanging by a thread. He had sustained three heart attacks and could succumb to another fatal one at any time, leaving her as the custodian of all his property.

My uncle turned his face to the left and furrowed his brow. The lightheartedness was replaced by a grim expression. The dagger was missing. And he knew exactly who had removed it. He strode toward the sofa, lifted the cushions. My grandmother had changed its hiding place.

Talk of the splendor and pomp of the past came to an abrupt stop. My uncle reprimanded his mother, demanding that she return the dagger to its place on the wall. He reprimanded her for not trusting her own son with the safety of his life. He reminded her that he had removed her from Lucknow for a more comfortable life. What could possibly happen to her? She was provided with the best medical treatment, the best food, the best neighborhood. Why was she paranoid? All this was said mostly in English with a British accent with a fair sprinkling of Hindi words pronounced like the British. If he had thrown a sheet over his face and body, he would have been taken to be British.

I'm not sure how much my grandmother understood of the volley of accusations he hurled at her. She was almost apologetic. She did not want to add anxiety to his already high-pressure life, but she feared for her life. Her voice trembled. Her eyes looked haunted by fear. The face, she claimed, continued to appear at the window; his estranged wife was trying to chase her out of the house by eyeing the dagger. This was not a delusion. How can I convince you?

She beckoned to me. "*Edhar aao* (Come here)." She patted at the cushion next to her. I moved close to her. She whispered, "Dolly, *ye aurat muje jeene nahi de gi* (This woman will not leave me alive). *Yeh mere jaan le le gi* (She will take my life)." She entreated me to convince my mother that her life was in danger.

I took my uncle aside and tried to convince him that his mother was not suffering from senility or delusion. She even remembered dates and years, her mother's birthday, important events in her father's life, and even facts about the mutiny. She was not incoherent. For her well-being, he should question his night guard about the mysterious man sneaking into the house. Also, he should consider locking the door on the inside of the house. It was not customary for a niece to lecture an uncle who was much older than she was. But I was deliberately flouting custom. I was returning to the US in a couple of days, and I didn't think anybody would give ear to her fears. Certainly not my mother. This was the tragedy of senility. Who could you trust?

My uncle looked at me as if I had also gone insane. There were now three mentally crazed women in the family. It was a madhouse. He, as the only sane male, reached out for his tumbler of whiskey and a cigarette to numb his mind of agitation and the emotional turmoil that the paranoia of two women had created. Drink followed drink; cigarette followed cigarette. The smoke stung my eyes and floated past our faces in disintegrating skeins. When I left, I had no doubt that my uncle would be sozzled by the evening and most certainly drunk by nighttime. My grandmother was right. She could not depend on him at night. She reported he was generally drunk. She also reported in a whisper to my mother that a woman of pleasure came once a week to visit him.

When I said goodbye and looked her consolingly in the eyes, I noticed that behind her head, there was an empty space where the dagger had been. My grandmother was a tenacious woman. She had been a pampered beauty used to giving orders, used to being obeyed. Nobody was going to convince her that she was imagining things. She would not submit to her son's exhortations. She would not be a party in her own murder. I recall my mother telling me that after the event of her murder, a month later, that her ghost was tenacious. It continued to haunt the house.

I was returned home in my uncle's car, speeding from the Greater Heaven No. 2 to Greater Heaven No. 1. In my mind, I was heading from one inferno to another. I mounted the steps slowly, arranging my face to meet my mother's. I wanted to communicate the urgency of my grandmother's conviction that she was being targeted for death.

My mother was waiting for me with a wary expression on her face. She was expecting bad news. She had wanted to protect me from a final meeting because she feared I would return to the US with a burdened heart. Sundari was in the kitchen; I could hear her fighting with the dishes. It sounded like the din of war.

I lay down on the bed and took a deep breath; I needed all my strength. "Mummy," I said, "if some years from now, you were convinced that your life was in danger, I would move you to my house till things were sorted out. If the notion was a fixation in your mind, I would take you to a psychologist. If the fear was genuine, I would take you to the police. Your mother has sent you an urgent message, '*ye aurat muje jeene nahi de ge* (that woman will not let me live). What are you going to do about this?"

"Your uncle won't let her move from his house. In India, it is the tradition for the son to take care of his mother. It will be a loss of face for him. What was his response to the fears your grandmother expressed?"

"He said they were unreal, figments of her imagination, a sign of dementia in senility."

"My sentiments exactly. Your grandmother likes drama. She likes to be the center of attention. This is one way she can command it. She has everybody, including you, in her web of morbid fancy."

"What if you're both in denial?"

"What if you're gullible? Hardheadedness and practicality was never your strength."

I got nowhere with my mother. All my efforts were a dead end. The unsaid message was that I was from a different generation and living in a different country. I did not understand Indian customs and traditions, and I should butt out. It was true that I gave people the benefit of the doubt and had been gulled into parting with money by stories concocted by charlatans, but I felt this was different. The heart's intuition cannot be wrong.

I shut my eyes and attempted to reconstruct every encounter I had had with my aunt from the time my uncle was married. This would throw some light on her character. I could then determine if she was the kind of woman who could stitch together a murder. Was she of the same ilk as Lady Macbeth, Clytemnestra, and Medea? Or was she a woman misunderstood? Was she a *femme fatale* or simply a modern cosmopolitan woman fighting for her rights and for self-determinism?

The first time I ever set eyes on her was at the age of thirteen. She arrived with my uncle to a house that had been cleaned, polished, and made fragrant for their arrival. The domestic staff was given a fresh uniform, and the children were told to be on their best behavior. Even my parents took extra care with their attire.

To my adolescent imagination, she was everything I would want to be as an adult: A glowing, peaches-and-cream complexion, dark, radiant eyes, their shape enhanced by mascara and eyebrow pencil, and perfect lips. I was bold enough to ask her the color of her lipstick. She said smilingly, "Wild Orchids." Her beauty made such an impression on me that now at seventy-eight, sixty-five years later, I still remember the color. She was full bodied, what one would call voluptuous. And, above all, she was modern. My hair, sadly, hung in two plaits below my waist. It was pulled back to prevent any waves or curls, which might encourage boys to whistle at me. Hers was in a stylish bob. When she flicked her back with a graceful tilt of the head, she resembled a Hollywood star.

This paragon of beauty had a present for me: A baby-blue jacket from Europe, the first foreign-made item of clothing I had ever owned. I was ecstatic; I thanked her like one mesmerized. My uncle, who pulled my plaits fondly, still had his army figure—broad-chested, flat-stomached, tall, and erect. He looked like a Norse hero; his thick hair slicked down, square jawed, and deeply suntanned. I noticed he had the "Misra" nose, the signature feature of the entire family.

After this brief interaction, I was asked to leave. My mother did not want me to see bottles of whiskey or vodka or the risqué shots of cabaret artists and other adult entertainment that my uncle had brought back from Europe. I sat outside the door with my ear plastered to the keyhole to hear the conversation. This was my first exposure to a truly modern couple who had actually toured Europe. This was the most exciting moment in my life.

What happened next shocked my sense of decency. I realized that everything that glitters was not gold. This paragon of beauty may have feet, not of clay, but something more earthy—dung. She came into my room, somewhat apologetically, and handed me a silk, heavily stained, menstrual garment to iron. It was a petticoat that was worn under the sari. I backed off in shock, then changed my mind, held the garment by the hem, and ironed about eight inches from the bottom. I placed it on her bed. By hindsight, the bloody petticoat foretold bloody happenings that would occur in the future.

The blood was a signature of things to come.

What kind of a person would ask for such a favor? Clearly, a shameless one. Why hadn't she washed her garment? It would have taken a couple of minutes. She was decidedly a careless and thoughtless woman. Why was she going to wear the stained garment for dinner? Because all she cared for was appearance. What was unseen did not matter. Why did she come secretly to my room? To avoid my mother and her reaction and to take advantage of a young girl who would oblige her. I felt used and filthy. When she appeared later wrapped in her brocaded silk, I was not impressed. I wondered if her seductive body held a diseased soul. In India, there are taboos around menstrual blood, so her indecent act did not sit lightly in my memory.

The rest of the evening, her tarnished image collected more dirt. She smoked incessantly, contradicted her husband vociferously, ate greedily, and even downed liquor copiously. This was a mannish woman, I decided. Someone who was not familiar with modesty, grace, tact, and sweetness, attributes that were prized in my family. I was relieved when the couple returned to Bombay.

There were some more minor encounters. None of them inspired affection in my heart. I felt she was like a cactus that had to be approached carefully, and I was the wrong person. Years later, we met in Nainital. Her marriage was on the rocks. She separated herself from the family and gazed at the mountains. My father coaxed me to approach her and to make her feel comfortable. When I attempted to draw her into our circle, she twisted her mouth in an ugly way. On another occasion, I observed my uncle and parents paging through handwritten aerogrammes that she had penned to her boss. From what I overheard, she had been planning to ensnare the boss by the use of her seductive powers to get her husband a raise. The incriminating letter was never and more found. My uncle had informed her that he was quite capable of earning a raise by his own effort, but she had insisted her feminine powers would move him up the ladder faster and more surely. Was she the classic *femme fatale*, the Delilah, the Loreie, or just an aggressively devoted wife, an ambitious vamp, a Lady Macbeth?

After I was engaged into a high-profile family, I had some casual encounters where hate against my mother and jealousy about my marriage was undisguised. It dripped from her face.

She even declared publicly, "I will break Dolly's marriage to teach her mother a lesson."

She spread rumors about my mother to poison my mother-in-law's mind. This ploy clearly hurt my marriage. Her black-magic-voodoo effort at my reception has already been described. She celebrated my divorce and expressed astonishment at how well I looked and how I had flourished after it. She had hoped I would be a broken woman. But as luck would have it, I grew wings. The way I see it, Oscar Wilde hit it on the head when he declared, "Divorces are made in heaven."

A predominant feature of her character was a one-upmanship, an ego that wanted to assert itself, that refused to be subordinate to anybody, that was unable to bow in humility or sustain injury with a spirit of forgiveness. Her motto was "Whatever you can do, I can do better." I remember how she yanked me away from her uncle's arms when he was teaching me a ballroom step, with a challenging, "I will teach her, not you." This tendency to assert herself in an almost mannish way made her competitive, vengeful, vindictive, unforgiving, and jealous. There are certain contexts where these attributes of dominance and control can act as virtues, for example, in competitive sports. Take for example, Muhammad Ali's description of himself in his autobiography, *My Own Story:* "I'm a fighter. I believe in the eye-for-an-eye business. I'm no cheek turner. I got no respect for a man who won't hit back. You kill my dog. You better hide your cat." This is all well and good, but a marriage is not a boxing match. In the domestic context gentleness, compromise, caring, and forgiveness are more appropriate, at least in families from Uttar Pradesh at that time.

This would also explain why my mother's urge to protect her brother, to advise her on matters of marriage, and to be critical of her pugnacious spirit, to request her to reign in her explosive fits of anger was especially displeasing to her. It led to a clash of wills.

What if her anger had curdled and she was ready to embark on a steeper version of herself to execute what was necessary to regain sovereignty of her property and assets?

CHAPTER 9

Passionate Sunsets

Every sunset brings the promise of a new dawn.
—Ralph Waldo Emerson

Sundari was preparing tea in the kitchen. In the past, tea would have involved much fuss with fine bone china, saucers, silver spoons, milk container, sugar container, and other genteel niceties. Nothing demonstrated my mother's changed circumstances than tea being poured in stainless steel glasses. My mother had disposed of all superficial extravagances. She was in survival mode.

Every evening, we sipped on our glasses of tea while watching the skies turn technicolor. It was like a free show. Sunsets were proof that no matter what happened during the day, it could end beautifully. Sunsets did not repeat themselves. The colors may have been the same, but the sweep, the streaks, the bars, the lines, the smudges always varied. In Western Maryland, where I lived, sunsets were a pastel watercolor painting. Baby-blue background with pearly bars, apricot streaks, a splash of deep pink, a pinprick of orange, a gentle bar of peach. All of it would gradually dissolve into smoldering embers and finally the shades of night.

In India, sunsets were much more passionate. Splashes of deep-grape juice purple, dashing orange and bloodred smudges competed to monopolize the sky. The sky was ablaze with brilliance. On my last night, it was brilliant with a stab of blood red and clouds of dusky purple, the color that a bruise leaves behind on the skin.

The sun was drowning in its own gold. It was time to leave my mother with my last words. But the best policy was to let her have her say.

"One advantage of the caste system was that a family was assured a commitment to attributes that were common to both parties," she reflected.

"Yes, I think that's universal. In the US, I can't see a Georgia girl harmonizing with a California boy, certainly not one from Berkeley or a girl from Alabama in a harmonious union with a boy from New York City. Marriage is hard enough without carrying the burden of disparate provinces and castes."

The people from Punjab and the people from Uttar Pradesh have values that are total opposites. Bluntness versus tact; extrovert versus introvert or balanced; vigorous versus lassitude; meat eaters versus vegetarians; bold versus cautious; loudmouthed versus diplomatic; extravagant versus conservative; showy versus modest...

"I get the idea," I said.

My mother's literary genius allowed her to recall these opposites at a moment's notice.

"Also, his wife was in her early thirties. Her personality was not malleable. Both their personalities were set," I added. "A full-blooded Sikh would have suited her. They could have exchanged blow for blow," I said, wondering what *Sikhs* would feel about my stereotyping them.

As a matter of fact, I was from the "genteel" province but, if pushed, could execute a punch worthy of a Punjabi woman.

"It's all destined," said my mother resignedly. "We who arranged the marriage, your father and I, were simply serving the couple their *karma*. We are not responsible. We were simply instruments in the hands of fate," declared my mother, washing her hands of all guilt.

Karma was a convenient catchall. It relinquished all parties of responsibility. The failure of my marriage was also attributed to *karma*. *Karma* was the whipping boy of Indian culture. It was the mule of which you mounted all your crimes then kicked the animal into the wilderness. I had a friend who married a man from India. She swore he used the word about fifty times a day. If he lost his wallet, it was *karma;* if he lost his job, it was *karma*; if he got a job, it was *karma*; if she aborted, it was *karma*; if she bore a child, it was *karma*. She wondered if he would name his son Karma. When they got divorced, *she* said it was *karma*.

Now it was time to say a few words. I reminded her that I was flying out of New Delhi the next morning. She would be on my mind. Her struggle after my father's death was downright heroic. To have a house standing, with the lower floor rented, was worthy of a medal. I compared her to Durga, the goddess of war, the Indian Athena, who rode a tiger while she upheld her lance and sword. We had strong women in our family, but senility had eroded their power and that the able-bodied needed to take care of the elderly ones. If, God forbid, her mother should meet her death by the hands of a stranger with an ex-daughter-in-law as the true executioner, how would she countenance the event?

"You will have deep remorse. You will be in anguish. You'll be heartbroken. Nothing will assuage your grief. Why don't you save yourself this torture of the soul by simply returning your mother from where she came? Take her to Lucknow."

"I can only take her if Sarla can accommodate her. If my brother agrees to part with her, if I'm strong enough to do it, if she agrees to go. One thing's for sure," she said, "if she leaves, the ex-wife will occupy the house on the pretext of her children's safety. She wants the mother out. Her dagger looks are a ploy to frighten the old woman."

I was left thinking that the bottom line was that my uncle could not handle the situation. He didn't have the guts; he wasn't forceful enough, not brutal enough. How could he be? Excessive drinking had eroded his masculinity. The equation was unequal: a degenerate man faced with a manly woman. Her poison was too potent for the likes of him. Had he used my mother all these years as a shield to fight an unruly woman? Had my mother acquiesced because she was the older sister who had always protected her younger brother? Was my weary, panic-stricken grandmother now protecting him from his revenge-seeking wife?

I did not voice my sentiments. My mother was sensitive about any criticism levelled against her brother. He had been her loyal protector growing up; she was his loyal admirer when he joined the army, and she was his shield now. She sometimes regretted how her handsome, heroic brother had succumbed to degenerate habits. She knew, as her mother did, that a woman of pleasure visited him a couple of times a week. Both mother and daughter simply averted their faces to the fact, just as they never addressed his heavy drinking.

Sundari came to my side to wish me farewell. I gave her enough money to refurbish her wardrobe. I reminded her that men can be scoundrels even if they were handsome and wore smart uniforms. I told her to be cautious and promised to teach her choice abuses in English on my next visit. There was one thing I didn't tell her: that women can also be scoundrels, even executioners, even though they did not wear smart uniforms.

She bowed a deep *namaste* and ran and said in a quiet voice, "*Aap bahut ache hai* (You're very nice)." Then she ran down the stairs to get her last glimpse of the man who had stolen her heart.

CHAPTER 10

A Letter Arrives

Our dead are never dead to us until we have forgotten them.
—George Eliot

I was back in Frostburg, a city in Allegheny County, Maryland, at the head of Georges Creek Valley, some miles from Cumberland. I lived in Finzel, a backwoods area of poor mountain people who resented the presence of an Indian in their midst. I noticed that everybody over thirty had their front teeth missing, nobody had an education past fifth grade; the men fixed their own secondhand trucks, the women grew their own vegetables. The area was rife with sex gossip, jealousy, and petty competition. No one liked anybody else, but all of them had one thing in common: They hated foreigners.

My slightly left-leaning cabin was situated on the crest of a hill with two tall pear trees, some apple trees, a lavender bush, and some evergreens that my children and I had planted to give us some privacy from the inmates of the rusted trailers who liked nothing better than to let the air out of my tires in the middle of winter. We had piled logs of hard wood that we used in our wood stove. We also had our own spring and a barn for a horse we didn't possess.

One cold winter day, I trudged up to the mailbox that was located on a street at some distance. Thrusting my hand into the snow-smothered mailbox, I retrieved a bunch of bills and a pale gray aerogram that I recognized as a letter from my mother. It was my habit to read all personal letters in my tiny loft, which had been an attic in the past that I had turned into my cozy bedroom. I slept on a single twin-size mattress laid flat on the wood-paneled floor with a tiny window just behind my head. This little window with its flying curtains acted as a spy hole. I could keep an eye on my children riding their bicycles in the summer and building their snowmen in the winter. My coal furnace and wood stove pumped hot air that rose to the loft and warmed my chilled bones in the winter. This, with my fluffy feather quilt and nubby sheep wool blankets, constituted my palace.

I piled my pillows against the wall, made myself comfortable, and prepared to open the aerogram. I noticed that one corner of the rectangle letter had been torn off. This is a practice in India to indicate bad news. It protects the heart from the effects of sudden shock. I furrowed my brow and held my breath in expectation. Had my mother fallen down the treacherous steps? Had her blood pressure led to a stroke? I imagined other horrific scenarios as I attempted to open the sealed aerogram. Indian paper does not hold out well; it crumbles to the touch. I needed to unseal the paper carefully, or I would lose the contents.

It was written in Hindi; my mother's literary style was always a pleasure to read. Her point of view was never commonplace, always convoluted. The first paragraph was about the changing weather; the second about her new manuscript and its prospective publisher. The third was about her impatience with the political wrangling and the stagnant nature of the economy. Finally, there was one stark line that translated as "You will be saddened to learn that your grandmother passed away." No details, no description of the impact, no mention of the funeral, no reference to her own grief. She might as well have said that there were no mangoes in the market or that the price of potatoes was steep. The sentence was as dry as a Euclid equation.

I called up my friend Vijay. He was from India, and I thought he may be able to clarify the anomaly. Was this also a tradition that in the first letter only one sentence be devoted to the deceased and a corner of the envelope be pinched off?

"Your mother may be saving herself grief. With her mother's death, it is the passing away of one generation. Now the grim reaper is approaching her own. This is not a smiling prospect. It's also possible that she wanted to spare you the details. She knows you have responsibilities and did want the fact of death to consume your energy."

Neither explanation applied. They were both out of character. My mother was stoical. Pain and suffering for her were the stuff of literature. Life was a game. She was a writer. It was natural for an elaborate description of the cremation to flow from her pen.

I phoned New Delhi.

Sundari answered, "Your mother is talking to a policewoman. She can't come to the phone. I have to hang up."

The phone went dead.

Why was she talking to a policewoman? Were the tenants downstairs acting up? Had the servant staff below bullied Sundari. The young girl often threatened them with the police.

I gave up. My upper body slid down the pile of pillows. I lay prone on my mattress. Memories from the past flooded my mind.

"This is a mysterious universe and impossible things happen," I told myself.

When my younger sister was nine years old, she contracted encephalitis and passed away in two days. My mother's grief was deep. She was inconsolable. My father was sobbing. Suddenly, from nowhere, my grandmother who lived in Lucknow, 334 kilometers away, appeared.

My mother gasped, "Mother, *aap kaha se aae* (Mother, where did you come from)?"

She looked around confused and questioned, "Has something happened?"

"Anu is dead," said my mother simply.

Her body lay on the ground, covered with a white sheet and overloaded with golden-colored marigolds. The doctors were devastated that they could not save her. The town was in shock. Rich and poor had collected on the lawns to pay their respects.

My grandmother's face collapsed. She burst into tears. "I was returning from your brother's house in Bombay. He suggested I go via Agra and see you. He bought my train ticket and insisted that I make a stop. So I'm here. I saw crowds of people in the lawn and crowds outside the gate. I thought you had thrown a party for the town. When did she die?"

"A couple of hours ago."

The two women clung together and sobbed. Was this a coincidence, or was it telepathy, or were their divine forces working behind the scene? G. K. Chesterton may have intuited this when he called coincidences "spiritual puns." The family must have been deeply connected at some level for my mother's brother who lived in Bombay to have arranged for their mother to stop at Agra en route to Lucknow. She arrived just before the body was taken for cremation. She was my mother's support and consolation in those sorrowful days.

I recall my own grief. I was about thirteen.

My mother said to me tearfully, "*Ab tumari koe bahan nahi rahi* (Now, you have no sister left)."

It was a simple sentence that I never forgot. There were many moments in my life when I wished I had a sister, and I would remember those poignant words.

I remembered my grandmother's sense of humor, her gift for narrating events with so much zest and detail that I felt I was witnessing them. This was a story about Sarla, my mother's younger sister. After the "misunderstanding," the switch in brides, Sarla left for London with her veterinarian husband for two years.

One day, her older brother, who did not speak English and scoffed at British pretensions, was standing at the window of his mother's upper-story house.

How is it that he spoke no English? I wondered.

"There were no English schools in Lucknow when he was born. He grew up to be a farmer and managed his mother's properties that she had received as part of her dowry."

He was at this time a young man and stood at the window of their double-story house enjoying the scene. Suddenly, his attention was directed to a girl seated in a rickshaw. He surveyed her from top to toe with cynical pleasure. She wore a smart hat, tilted stylishly to one side; her lipstick was a deep hibiscus red. She had a form-fitting jacket, a tight knee-length skirt, ultra-smooth stockinged legs, and high-heeled shoes. She sat with her legs to the side and her torso drawn up. She looked like a perfect imitation of a young British woman.

He surveyed her from top to bottom and exclaimed to himself in the rough vernacular of the day, "What a sight! All togged up, thinks she is God's gift to mankind. Hell, what a fake! I want to laugh, but I can't take my eyes off her."

Unexpectedly, the rickshaw changed direction and came directly under his window. He fell back in surprise.

"Was this jezebel actually visiting someone in this genteel neighborhood? Who on earth would entertain this painted fake?"

The rickshaw turned right onto the side street leading to his house. He gagged. "This overdressed wretch is entering our compound? Am I seeing right?"

There was a knock at the door. He opened the door and fell back flabbergasted, clutching his breast. His eyes opened wide; his jaw dropped.

"Is that you, Sarla? What happened to you? Is that really you?"

"Why, brother, don't you recognize me? I'm your sister, Sarla. I'm paying a surprise visit."

My grandmother would embroider the details lovingly, imitating her son's voice as he scoffed and spewed out profane comments. She would also imitate his astonishment that the girl was his own younger sister. She would roll her eyes and pretend to hyperventilate. We would titter and giggle falling over each other. The Sarla we knew was firmly rotund and imagining her in a knee-length skirt and a hat tickled our funny bone.

I thought of my grandmother's letters that my mother would read out to us.

After an unceasing rain pour flooded Lucknow, she wrote in Hindi, "Our roads have become rivers and our automobiles have become boats. I stand at my window and watch boatmen lift drowning bodies out of the water and carry them to safety. There are boats floating around the house. This is a new landscape."

She could read faces.

During the *vida* (leaving home) at my wedding, she came up to me close and whispered, *"Hoshyari se rahna."*

Hoshyari has a special meaning. It is something between shrewdness, cautiousness, and cleverness. She was telling me to be alert, not to be naive or gullible. My mother reported later that she whispered in her ear that my prospective father-in-law looked like a grave and honorable man, but my prospective mother-in-law's eyes had a sly and cunning look. She could not be trusted.

Time would prove her right. Her fears about the dagger on the wall was also based on the threatening or more bluntly murderous look on the face of the estranged wife.

She loved to remind us that along with her British nanny who taught her how to knit, crochet, and embroider; she also had a maid who dressed her. She called the application of cosmetics and the wearing of jewelry *shringar*. *Shri* is the name of *Lakshmi*, the goddess of beauty and prosperity. The wearing of cosmetics and ornaments celebrates the beauty and divinity of the female form. It transforms what in the West is a secular activity and a cosmetician a professional like any other into a divine art form presided over by *Lakshmi*, the goddess of beauty.

On special occasions, such as festivals and an event such as a marriage, the maid would complete the *solah shringar* (sixteen ornaments). I can still remember the Hindi names of what I considered "armor of gold." Completely dressed, these sixteen ornaments could heighten the charms of a beautiful girl into a celestial beauty and a plain girl into an attractive damsel.

Some of these ornaments had been gifted to my mother as part of her dowry. I had seen her wear the *tagri*, a gold belt with sculpted pieces of gold linked together with a chain. Each piece had *Saraswati*, the goddess of learning, embossed in the center. She was seated on a lotus holding a sitar, her musical instrument. Each was embossed with an identical motif. There was the *gulband*, a three-inch band resplendent with diamonds on gold. This was worn on the upper arms. The gold bangles that encased the arms from the wrist to the elbow were called *bajuband*. Then there were *payjeb* for the ankles that made sweet music when women walked. The footwear was made of velvet with *sitare* and *salma* (sequins). There were necklaces, each identified with a specific name. What I enjoyed especially playing with was the *nath*. This was a nose ring. They came in several sizes. My grandmother had a gold one of some eight inches. It was delicate with the tiniest of bells and iridescent beads. All ornaments in India are related to health in some way. My grandmother explained that the sixteen *shrigars* corresponded to the sixteen phases of the moon, which in turn was connected with a woman's menstrual cycle. They would also nullify the negative effects of that cycle. Ear and nose piercings were related to the health of the kidney and the bladder, and toe rings and anklets were related to the nervous system. Some ornaments protected a woman from the damaging effects of the evil eye.

My mother had gifted me her *jhumkas* (hanging earrings) that were so heavy that they required a fine gold cord that looped behind the ears to hold them in place. I kept mine in a blue, velvet pouch. My grandmother had worn them, and my mother and I would pass them to my daughter.

The wind was howling outside. The coal furnace required some fresh shovels of coal; the wood furnace required some logs. As I descended the stairs from my loft, I kicked my leather boots aside. How different my life was from my grandmother's. Good, fresh, lumpy coal, a shovel, a poker, a bucket to remove ashes, gloves, a supply of kindling, old newspapers, and cardboard were more important for my survival than the gold of all sixteen ornaments of the *solah srinagar.*

I descended the dusty steps to the basement that I called the inferno.

"I bet," I told myself, warming to the subject, "I could name sixteen items related to my coal furnace."

As I shoveled coal that had been moved from the mountain of the precious black to the stove with my shovel laden with giant coal rocks, I bounced my stove specific vocabulary off: ashpan, flu pipe, creosote, kindling, Anthracite coal, Bituminous coal, grate, kindling, masonry chimney. The list was short of sixteen, but I could tell how long forty pounds of coal would burn on a cold December night like this one, and I could... A sudden wave of heat raised a shower of glowing embers to the mouth of the furnace. Startled, I backed away. I could also survive the operation three times a day with minor burns when I forgot to wear my gloves.

I removed my coal-stained apron and hung it on its hook. I removed my padded gloves and stuck them in the pockets of the apron. Then I started my trek back to my cozy attic, shuffling slowly in my sheep-lined bedroom slippers.

Throwing myself onto my feather quilt, I asked myself: "Is my grandmother really dead if I can recall her words, her humor, her letters, her jewelry in every detail?"

People die when we forget them. And my memoir, a modest, clumsy effort, could, if it resonated in the hearts of my readers, make her immortal. Grandmothers don't die, nor do they fade away like generals; they live in the photographs on our walls and the letters we have preserved in our desks. They live in the stories that we pass on to our children and they to their children. They are immortal.

The stove was doing its magic, the air from the cracks of my secondhand window frame was reminding me of the cold night air outside, but I wrapped myself in my feather quilt and consoled myself with Tagore's words, "Death is not extinguishing the light; it is only putting out the lamp because the dawn has come."

Tomorrow will be another day.

CHAPTER 11

Return to India

Truth may sometimes appear to be unpalatable and unreasonable.
But ultimately, it finds its own way to establish itself.
—Nihar Satpathy

"The man who passes the sentence should swing the sword. If you would take a man's life, you owe it to him to look into his eyes and hear his final words. And if you cannot bear to do that, then perhaps the man does not deserve to die."

It was 1990, two years since the death of my grandmother. I was preparing to return to India for my yearlong sabbatical. My mother had remained close-lipped about any details of my grandmother's death. Her letters focused on the excitement of moving to the lower story. She had won her case against her troublesome tenants, had ousted them, was moving to occupy the marble-finished floors of the spacious rooms, and was looking forward to my visit. Her motto was life is for the living. I arrived at the newly furbished New Delhi airport and elbowed my way through the pressing crowd, straining to exit from the gate where I would see a driver holding up my name. And indeed, I caught my name inked in black on a white banner. The letter "*E*" of my first name was reversed with the three prongs facing left. I had to smile. The driver holding the banner and another youth, a nondescript who was unable to introduce himself, walked ahead leading me toward the car.

So my mother now had a mansion and a chariot. This was progress. She also had a driver who had an aide. The car was a tiny, gray, square tin box, a Fiat made in India. It had a rooftop. This would become its identifying feature in a parking lot in the days to come. The two men unrolled a thick rope, hoisted my suitcases to the rooftop, and positioning themselves on either side of the car, tightened the ropes, throwing it back and forth. The driver then handed me a flask of fresh water. I felt I was in a desert, slaking my thirst and waiting to hoist myself on a camel. There was a third world feel to the operation.

That Fiat stayed with my mother for some twenty-five years. In future years, I would see her on one side of the car with the mechanic on the other. She would watch with an eagle eye as he fixed, replaced, or tightened a malfunctioning part. She could name all the basic parts of an engine: crankshaft, piston, camshaft, cylinder head, spark plug, valves, sump, and so on. This working knowledge would allow her to make sure that while fixing one part of the engine, the mechanic did not steal another. This was a habit of mechanics. Gardeners were known for a similar pilfering. It was necessary to count all the plants to make sure that the gardener did not replace in his pocket a seedling while preparing a bed for a fresh planting. She was nobody's fool.

In later years, with the wear and tear, this Fiat would look like a dented, senile wreck but always a functioning wreck. It had grit. It could rise from its ashes. After my mother passed away in 2016 and no clunker appeared at the airport, I thought of her shabby jalopy with tearful eyes. While she was alive, somebody had cared enough for me to provide transportation. After her death, I had to use the impersonal taxi.

My mother was waiting on the front porch. The wind had sneaked up her petticoats and ballooned her sari into a billowing wave. The sparrows were pecking at the scattered corn, and some tall bamboo fonds were waving in the wind. In my family, nobody kissed or embraced. We just looked languishingly at each other, patted each other's back, mumbled greetings, and continued with commonplace pleasantries. The welcome was always anemic in outward robustness, but it was stoically heartfelt.

I was taken on a tour of the house. My mother was living in style again. Her characteristic way of arranging furniture and decorative items was evident. An entire room now served as her prayer room. The gods were no longer cramped uncomfortably in a corner. They could saunter across the room at leisure. The house was fragrant with incense. A welcome *kum kum* (a red powder used ceremonially) mark was affixed to my forehead.

We sat on cane chairs on the front porch, sipping tea from fine china cups. The crockery had been upgraded. Sundari had been replaced by a smart, Western-dressed girl from Assam. When I questioned my mother about Sundari, an expression of emotional exhaustion and pain suffused her face.

"We'll talk about that later. I may write a story about her. I miss her fresh, forthright nature. This one is demure and very correct in her ways."

She talked as though she was distracting herself from a subject she was trying to avoid. Gradually, the life in her voice petered out. Her voice became crumbly. Her breathing became labored. With eyes half-closed.

She spoke in a low moan, "Your grandmother was murdered."

There was a long painful pause.

"How...Who...Why...Where?" The questions tumbled out from my heaving chest. "Why was I told nothing? Was the murderer apprehended?" It seemed my questions would never cease. It was easier to question than to sit quietly with a heavy heart.

"She was stabbed by a dagger," said my mother. Her eyes took on a haunted look.

"Was this the dagger on the wall? Was this the dagger that she used to hide?"

"Yes."

"Was the murderer the dark face that peered into her room at night?"

"Yes."

"Was he apprehended? Is he in jail?"

"He was apprehended, but he jumped out of a moving train and could not be taken into custody."

"Wasn't he handcuffed? How could he jump out? Why wasn't he followed?"

There was silence. My mother looked tired, as though she was carrying a great weight on her shoulders. She was bowed and ready to fall over. Wisps of hair had disengaged from the knot at the back of her head. Her glasses were ready to slide down her nose.

"Take me to my bed. I need to lie down," she whispered. "I'll tell you the story some other time. You rest also. You must be exhausted."

I reclined on a lounge chair. Thoughts raced through my mind. My grandmother had been right all along, and nobody believed her. Poor woman: all her gold could not save her; it became the cause of her death. She concealed the weapon. Still it was found out. There was no dodging death. On the occasion of my uncle receiving the award of arms from the king of Nepal, could he have ever imagined that the embossed handled dagger would be the cause of his beloved mother's death? The irony was staggering. How did my uncle respond to the death? Where was the mentally sick Vimla? Did she let out a cry? These were questions my mother needed to answer. Now that she had broken news of the most shocking core deed, the rest would be easier. The knife thrust of the event had been endured. The rest was discussion on the subject, a kind of anatomy of the murder.

I brushed my hair out of my face impatiently and smudged the *kum kum* into a grainy red smudge on my forehead. The ceremonial rice grains scattered in my hair. At least the suspense was over. At least the silence was broken. On the first day of my last visit, I was informed by my terrified grandmother of the likelihood, no, actually the assurance of her murder. This was the first day of my second visit. I was now informed that it had been consummated successfully.

In a couple of hours, my mother was up and about. We were back on the front porch. In one corner of the twenty-feet-by-twenty-feet-sized garden was a large pile of aqua-colored rocks, almost the size of a small hillock, that looked out of place in a tropical climate and in a lush garden with a bamboo grove in one corner. These rocks were from Gangotri, a pilgrimage place on the banks of the River Bhagirathi and origin of the River Ganges. It is on the Greater Himalayan Range, at a height of 3,100 meters. They had been brought down by jeep way back in the past during one of my father's tours in Uttarakhand. They reflected the color of the glaciers and the frothy water. My mother had carried these rocks with her belongings from house to house. In an enclosed space indoors, there were two plaques with the names of two esteemed gurus. They had laid the first stone on the day of the sod-turning ceremony on the first day of construction. The house was built on sacred ground.

We inhaled the perfume of night blooming jasmine and settled down for a less than fragrant conversation. I was impatient to hear the who, what, when, how of what had transpired. The questions were tumbling out in a disorderly jumble. I reigned in the uncontrollable momentum and opened with the first obvious question: How was it done?

The police report stated that a man broke in late at night when everybody was asleep. He did not have to break the lock because the inside *kundi* (a heavy latch on the door in Indian homes) located at the summit of the door had been released. This made the entry of the intruder convenient. The dagger was then removed from the wall. Your grandmother was first suffocated then stabbed with the dagger. There was some blood. Her cash, gold bangles, and keys were not removed from under her pillow nor was a single object removed from the wall.

"Vimla, my mentally disturbed sister, continued to sleep, and your uncle in the next room also slept undisturbed. After the man completed the deed, he leaned against the wall to catch his breath, and pressed his blood-stained hand against the white wall to hold his balance. This left a clear imprint on the wall, which the police were able to photograph."

"Who undid the bolt?"

"There are four suspects: a disgruntled domestic, his estranged wife, my mentally handicapped sister, or my brother who carelessly left the door open when he returned home at night."

"Did they recover the dagger?"

"The dagger was left standing upright in my mother's heart."

"And the man?"

He was apprehended and handcuffed but escaped by jumping from a running train. The case was in the hands of a senior police officer who was married to my younger sister. He was my brother-in-law. There may have been some exchange of money to prevent the case from being divulged. After the murder, the objective was not to apprehend the culprit but to prevent the truth from being divulged. It was to save face.

I was shocked with this new convolution of a bribe given to affect a cover-up. My mother, sometime later, called it "a gift of money" because the officer was his own brother-in-law. But it amounted to the same thing.

I was looking at the glacier-colored rocks. The sparrows were hopping at the summit and a crow was harassing them. They would unite in guerrilla fashion and charge the crow. There was aggression and strife in all aspects of nature, and human life was no different. In the snow-covered Himalayan peaks with the clear waters of the Ganges flowing in a broad stream, the rocks strewn along the borders were always perfectly reflected in the flowing water, but in the plains, the Ganges lost its transparency. In like manner, in everyday life, truth existed on the peaks and in the hearts of saints in deep meditation, but in the filth and grime of common life, it covered its face. What was reflected is what people wanted the world to see. In the words of Garcia Marquez, "A lie is more comfortable than doubt, more useful than love, more lasting than truth."

My mother agreed with me. "What we have now is not the truth but arguments about different versions of a lie. The tact required to preserve civility in life along with the profit and utilitarian concerns teaches people how to cover up the truth and how to believe in lies. What really happened is inconsequential, what we hear is different sides—my side, his side, their side, the media's side. The truth is a corpse."

I thought of all the books written about scandals of celebrities, the assassinations of presidents, of bribes given and taken; they were mostly theories of what happened. Who assassinated Kennedy? Was Lal Bahadur Shastri, the Prime Minister of India, 1964, assassinated secretly? What about Martin Luther King and Mahatma Gandhi?

And what about Indra Gandhi? Malcolm X? Thomas Sowell's insight resonates at this moment: "There are only two ways of telling the truth—anonymously and posthumously." And I might add that even that can be muffled till eons have passed and nobody cares, and nobody has anything to lose. The truth is a corpse, but the lie will be dissected, rehashed, altered, debated ad nauseum.

When you talk with members of the family, what you will hear are perceptions, I reflected. Each member will try to protect his or her honor by removing himself or herself from the equation. Each one will try to appear blameless or on the periphery. The murder is now gossip. It is the talk of Delhi. It was on the cover page of *The Times of India.* The estranged ex-wife was the main suspect. But she is now out of the picture.

"The suspicion is on blameless people who cannot defend themselves: A domestic cook and my mentally challenged sister. The first is poor and illiterate. The second's mind is a blank sheet. Nobody knows what's on her mind, not even herself. Posterity will remember her as a criminal, even though this mad aunt kept the true criminal out of jail. The truth has been murdered and buried. Voiceless idiots are the new suspects. They would compromise nobody's honor. Thoughts such as these troubled my mind."

My attention was arrested by the uniformed, stalwart driver washing the car on the side of the street across from the climbing hibiscus, which we in India called *gudhal ke phool,* which covered the wall separating my mother's house from the neighbor's. These flowers were dear to the goddess Durga. At her prayer time, she would lay two red hibiscus flowers at the goddess' feet. In traditional India, women would make a paste with the leaves and wash their hair. The oil in the leaves made a perfect hair conditioner.

But on this occasion, the flowers and the driver reminded me of Sundari.

"Why did she leave? She was a good worker and was learning to write in Hindi and English."

My mother put her hands through her hair and took a deep breath.

"That driver there broke the poor girl's heart. In the labor class, drivers occupy a prestigious position. While gardeners and cooks have to dirty their hands and perform common work such as growing vegetables, cutting carrots, and grinding spices, drivers are analogous to chariot drivers. They would drive the king's chariot across the city. Now automobiles have taken the place of the chariot and the engine the place of horses. But the prestige remains. For a domestic servant to be betrothed to a driver is analogous to a commoner marrying an IIT graduate. He thought her below his status and scoffed at her plain face and rough speech."

"So what happened?"

My mother described how, one morning, there was a knock at the door. She opened it and fell back in astonishment. There was a young woman standing dressed in a lavender-colored sari with shimmering silver jewelry to match. Every detail of her apparel matched the color of the sari. Her hair was done up in a bun with lavender flowers entwined along the side tresses. She was in heels.

"Memsahib, don't you recognize me? I'm Sundari."

"Sundari, what happened to you? I thought a Bollywood actress had come to visit me."

"I am coming from a beauty salon. They took three months of my salary to do my makeup. I want you to take my marriage proposal to the driver. I know he loves me. I am dressed for the betrothal."

"But, Sundari, he will never agree. He has his sights on girls from richer families."

"No, I know he will marry me. Just take my proposal. I beg you to take my proposal. I have no one to do it," she pleaded with tears in her eyes.

In order to humor her, I phoned my neighbor and told her my predicament: "My domestic help is infatuated with your driver. Can you ask him if he's willing to get betrothed?"

The lady of the house shook with laughter. "He'll never agree, but I will ask him and get back with you."

Sundari sat on a chair in suspense, holding her lavender purse in her hand. The mistress of the neighboring house called after half an hour. She said the driver was insulted to be approached by a *chokri* (a young, common girl, not a lady). He told her to "buzz off."

My mother broke the bad news to Sundari very gently, but she shed copious tears. Her carefully applied mascara spread all over her roughed cheeks. She left with head bowed and never returned.

"It happens in the best of families," I muttered.

I slept fitfully, conscious for some moments and in a hellish sleep for some hours, then back to a restless waking state. My waking and sleeping were disturbed with phantasmagoric images, some derived from reality and other from drama. My mind felt like a horror theater with an unseen hand projecting frightening images. It seemed that tragic plays such as *Macbeth, King Lear,* and *Julius Caesar* took on a significance far beyond literary horror. The lines spoke to me; they were written with a finger dipped in blood.

Lady Macbeth, wringing her guilt-ridden, blood-stained hands with mutterings of, "Out damned spot... Who would have thought the old man to have had so much blood in him?"

The wretched woman desperate to get the smell of blood out of her hands, fearing that all the perfumes of Arabia would fail to expel the stench of her guilt. I had acted the part of Lady Macbeth in a college play in the 1960s. The poignant lines were deeply entrenched in my memory as the fitful walking back and forth of a hysterical woman whose conscience was racked by guilt and whose imagination could only project the smell of blood and blood-dripping images.

When Lady Macbeth receded from my restless sleep, Julius Caesar, the Roman dictator, took her place. It was the Ides of March, Caesar was seated, crowned, and robed in scarlet as in Karl von Piloty's painting. A roman senator is depicted pulling on Caesar's toga to distract and pin him down as Servilus Casca sneaks behind Caesar and attempts to stab Caesar with a dagger. In my nightmare, the toga took on the folds of a *sari* (traditional dress of Indian women), and the senator's coloring changed to a deep suntan. The thrust of the dagger was repeated again and again as blood spurted and covered the assailant's hand.

Somebody was shaking me.

"*Utho, utho* (Wake up, wake up). *Koi bhayanak sapna* (a terrifying dream)?"

It was the maid. Her face looked terrified.

"*Aap cheek rahi thee* (You were howling)." She mopped my brow and commented on the sweat beaded on my forehead. She handed me a glass of water. "*Do baje hai, aaram se soiye* (It's two o'clock, sleep restfully)."

I took some deep breaths and shut my eyes. How could I keep these bloody images from wrecking my peace of mind?

What followed was even stranger. I was in a half-sleep. My grandmother walked into the theater of my mind. She looked composed but wore a severe expression on her face as though she was going to pass judgement.

"*Why are you polluting your mind with hysterical-inducing images and other people's opinions? Examine the facts. I am the victim. I was murdered. Do you want to hear what I have to say? Or do you want to rely on people's opinions—your mother's, your uncle's, your brother's, the policewoman, the chief of police? I am the ghost of the murdered woman. Onlookers can rationalize murder, but the victim knows its horror.*

"*They did not believe me in life, why should they believe me in death? When I was alive, they would not move me to Lucknow, a safe place. They brushed off my fears as hallucinatory. I was a senile woman whose perception could not be trusted. Why didn't they address my fears? I'll tell you why. It was inconvenient to move me, just too much trouble. It would hurt my son's reputation. Better to nurse his ego, his reputation, than to address my fears.*

"*What are they doing in death? Exactly the same thing. It's too troublesome, too harrowing to go through an authentic investigation. What would people say if the real culprit was apprehended? What would it do to my son's reputation? It would dishonor the family. What honor are they trying to protect when they have none? My death is inconvenient for them, as was my life. They brushed my fears under the carpet, and they will brush my death under the carpet.*

"*I have been removed from the scene. The family must fight my case. Do they have the courage? Do they have the guts? Have I raised a bunch of self-serving cowards? Have I suckled these hypocrites on my breasts?*

Is this how they repay me? They showed no manhood when I lived, and they demonstrate no manhood in my death. I thought I gave birth to five daughters and two sons. I now know they're all eunuchs. They're all cheap politicians. Their language is designed to make a bloody deed look respectable. They will make nonsensical ideas look solid. They will take a harmless lamb such as Vimla and give her a murderous heart and bloody hands while the true black-hearted culprit is allowed to escape.

"You, my son, fought in World War Two and murdered thousands to the sound of bugles and trumpets. You were awarded medals. But you cannot protect your ageing mother? You made a feast of blood. The newspapers published your exploits. We framed photographs of you in uniform. You fought to protect the world at the cost of your life. But you could not protect your mother? I was stabbed by your own ammunition that hung on the wall as a decoration.

"Mark my words: If you trade your authenticity for safety, you will die of grief. Your heart will not stay lodged in its cradle, it will rise up and strangle you."

The apparition melted into the night.

My grandmother had stripped the family of its slime of hypocrisy. She had stated in naked words that hypocrisy had taken the place of sincerity.

There was no sleep for me. I walked out of the room onto the patio. It was still dark.

The heavy perfume of the hyacinth suffused the air. It had always surprised me how nature continued in its workings, even in the starkest tragedies. The sun would rise, a digit at a time, the birds would waken with the dawn, and the hyacinth would continue to exude perfume, irrespective of who stood by its bush, murderer or saint. Nature made no distinctions.

The guard who was supposed to protect my mother's house was in a deep sleep. The job of security guard was just an income for him. He would get all the sleep he could steal. On one of my late-night excursions, I had to climb the wall to get into the house while he remained snoring on the settee.

My grandmother must have been offered the same protection, I mused. *The murderer sneaked through the gate as he had done in his past "dry runs," tiptoed into the living room through the unbolted door, removed the dagger from the wall, suffocated my mother with his brawny experienced hands, thrusted the dagger into her heart, and rested by leaning against the wall.*

"Murder," as Satre commented, "is extremely exhausting." To his observation, I would add, "Investigating the truth is more so." Only poorly planned murders are solved; those well planned require courage, patience, integrity, which can be defined as a dedication to the truth. These virtues were in short supply.

It was said of Het Ram, my great-grandfather, that he would not lie even if it cost him his life. His impeccable integrity was recognized by the British. "I would trust him like my own right hand," said one letter of recommendation. What was passed on to his grandchildren was not his integrity but his money.

CHAPTER 12

Negligence and Shame

Always the victor writes the history of the vanquished.
He who beats distorts the faces of the beaten. The weaker
depart from this world and the lies remain.
                                                    —Bertolt Brecht

What you see and what you hear depends on where you are
standing. It also depends on what sort of person you are.
                                                    —Anonymous

My mother was up with the dawn. Her most cherished moments were to sit in her garden and enjoy the aqua color of her glacial rocks, the perfect roundness and the orange color of her mandarin oranges, and the quick, chirping, flickering motion of her sparrows. A day before she passed away in 2011, she asked for her bed to be moved to the front porch, so she could have a view of the garden and her sparrows. At that time, I quoted Catullus's lines to her, "Better a sparrow living or dead, than no bird song at all." She was too far gone to understand, but a vague smile flickered on her face.

This morning was no different, except the quote was uttered from her mouth: "Look at the sparrow," said Mahatma Gandhi. "They do not know what they will do the next moment. Let us literally live from moment to moment." She scattered bird cereal in the turf and sat down to enjoy their happy pecking. Her final commitment was to her God.

She plucked two hibiscus flowers and disappeared indoors to her prayer room. Pain was of our making, but the endurance of it was mostly in His hands, even though a sparrow must "needs be a hawk to survive." We had breakfast on the front patio. The sparrows were pecking at their cereal, and we were forking our *cheelas*. *Cheelas* are the Indian variety of pancakes made of washed *moong* lentils and rice, soaked overnight. They taste delicious with yogurt and mint chutney. We could hear the sound of bells and religious music blaring from the *Ram* Temple. Hindu priests appeared to be in competition with the Muslim *mullahs* (religious teachers of Islam). In Islamic countries, it was the practice to recite the *Quran* over loudspeakers, to announce morning prayers for communal gatherings. One could tell if a town had a predominantly Muslim community or a Hindu one by the deafening music or recital over loudspeakers. Our neighborhood was decidedly Hindu. My mother hummed along with the music and clapped her palms together in rhythm.

At such times, she was reluctant to talk about earthly matters of the sordid kind—money, sex, divorce, and other social pathologies. It was her practice to tear out and discard the corner portion of *The Times of India* that advertised a heavily made-up woman with swelling breasts and luxuriant hair, selling some product or advertising the fake charms of Bollywood. She thought the vulgar photographs polluted the freshness of the morning and the enjoyment of reading her favorite paper. Her interest in politics and the news was a lifetime passion. I remember reading the paper to her one day before she died. I could imagine her sadness on reading about her mother's murder on the front page of her favorite paper.

But I required some answers, especially after my restless night. She had lived with the event for over two years and had hashed it to death with the rest of the family. They had exhausted the subject, but the jolt was still new to me. I had on my visits in the past noticed a certain complacency in her family, a kind of inertia that I felt contributed to Vimla's mental derangement, her father's death of kidney failure, and now her mother's murder. It was a sensitive subject. In the past, I had heard her defend her family against any allegation of a negative kind.

"Mummy," I said, in a low, empathic voice, "do you think that negligence may have contributed to the sorry state of affairs? I remember you attributing Vimla's failure to recover from emotional trauma to your parents not following the protocol. The psychiatrist had recommended that she be kept away from Lucknow and her home for a year, but she returned after a couple of months."

Her mind receded back into the old grooves, her emotional wound returned and there was no healing.

"Yes," she said readily, "after my father's retirement, there was a change in the family atmosphere. The intellectual ferment dissipated, and a complacence took its place. There was not much social interaction and little stimulation of any kind."

"My sentiments exactly," I piped in, relieved to note there was no resistance. "I think your father's death was also premature. His kidneys were malfunctioning, but the condition was kept secret."

"You may have a point there," she said meditatively. "He has only come once in my dream after his death. He gave me this message: *Mera ilaj thik nahi hua* (My medical treatment was inadequate). Your father and I did get him treated, but it was much too late. We had not been informed on time. His condition was kept secret from the public."

"D'you think that your mother's tragic end was mostly negligence? D'you think that if the issues had been addressed on time, the tragedy could have been averted as in the other situations? She expressed her fears. She concealed the dagger. She described the venomous looks that her ex-daughter-in-law directed at her. She even confided her fears to me. She told you that 'this woman' will not let me live, but none of her fears were addressed. Once again there was apathy and complacency—anything to avoid action or to disturb the status quo."

I remembered reading in an anthropology text that civilizations are either shame/honor cultures or guilt cultures and that India and all of South Asia belonged to the first category: shame/honor. In shame cultures, the sin is not of much importance or the dictates of conscience; what is of vital importance is the reputation of the person. The Hindu language has several words to describe this attribute, each with a slightly different nuance: *izzat, sharafat, nam/ badnaam, maan, aadar, sharam, lajja,* and others that I cannot recall at the moment. To lose one's reputation and honor in India is to be a social outcast.

I have some experience with this kind of isolation. A prosperous man who lived some houses from my mother's house had been identified as a pedophile by the neighborhood. Gossip about him was rife. The newspaper also carried the allegation and the legal implications. While I was in India, he threw a party for the neighborhood. Not a single person showed up.

Violations of traditional mores such as losing one's virginity before marriage, adultery, rape, divorce, theft, embezzlement of money, gross disregard for one's parents, cheating, and other gross misbehavior was not tolerated by society. Thus if a violation occurred in a family, it was imperative that secrecy be maintained. This secrecy also extended to mental illness, disease, and other disabilities. It was difficult to negotiate a marriage if people had wind of mental illness or diseases in the family. Thus the need for secrecy often interfered with families seeking medical help or therapeutic help for psychological problems till it was too late.

My mother agreed that this factor of maintaining appearances at any cost was a factor in the flouting of my grandmother's pleas for help. The divorces in the family were shameful enough. To move my grandmother back to Lucknow or even to my mother's house would imply that a son of the family was not capable of protecting his mother. If word had got around that the ex-wife was a threat to a ninety-year-old mother, the possibility of opprobrium would have been exacerbated. It would make him look like a wimp.

But my mother made one distinction, "My brother was a modern man. Social stigma mattered but not to the extent that it would to a conservative man living in the fifties. In his case, it was more a loss of face in his relationship with his mother and the family. He wanted to play the role of a hero, someone who would stand by his mother no matter what. He was sincere in this. But his quirky situation as a newly divorced man with an ex-wife hell-bent on revenge and on acquiring his property and assets and his weakness for alcohol put him in a situation that was untenable.

"He sounds like a tragic hero," I said, suddenly seeing him in a different light.

"Yes, I would say so," agreed my mother. "If you had seen the expression on his face at the time that they were carrying his mother's body out of his house, you would have believed the impact of her death. He had covered her body with flowers that would have been enough for three corpses. His face was purple with rage. His eyes were restraining an outpouring of tears. He was restraining himself, which added to the painful tension on his face. He had failed his mother, and he would not forgive himself." She added that he was from a Western, elitist public school, the most expensive in India. His mores were more conscience directed.

Indian traditions were more of a veneer; they were not integral to his character.

My mother had given me much to think about. Things were not as they seem. Her brother was not exactly "chameleon-ing" his way through life. I postponed questions about her perception of her own role in this tragedy for the day following. Both of us needed to relax, and we thought a silent walk in the park would revive our spirits.

CHAPTER 13

Points of View

Controllers, abusers, and manipulative people don't question
themselves. They don't ask themselves if the problem is
them. They always say the problem is someone else.

—Darlaene Ouimet

The next morning, I planned to talk to my brother, a cousin, and aunt about the event. In the interests of objectivity, it was imperative that I move beyond the lockhole of my own fixation and my mother's opinions and consider the point of view of others. To take a fixed position is analogous to the rigor mortis of the inquiring mind. Flexibility and an open mind are the elements of a living entity. I was astonished at the different versions of the incident. The truth may be one, but it is a prism that refracts people's perceptions into differing versions of the truth or different versions of the lie.

My first station of inquiry was a visit to my brother's house. He was a senior diplomat in the Indian Foreign Service and was not likely to get lost in the labyrinthine darkness of the incident. Even before I broached the subject, I could tell from the expression on his face that he found the subject unpalatable and in his deft, diplomatic way, moved it toward an early termination. It has been said of diplomats that they think twice about everything and say nothing about anything. I'll credit my brother with one word on the subject: "Mystery."

"We don't know what happened. It's a mystery."

"But who was the perpetrator of the crime?" I insisted. "Who was likely to benefit from snuffing out the life of a ninety-year-old woman?"

"I just said it's a mystery. The definition of mystery is that the facts are unknown. Family members, such as our mother, have theories, the police have their suspicions, but the reality is shrouded in darkness. You'll save yourself much heartache if you simply accept that what happened is a mystery. A mystery is a not-knowing and a willingness to be at ease with it. Case closed."

I could tell he was done with the subject, but reading my mind, he added as an afterthought: "Believe me, the ex-wife looked as baffled as the rest of us. She wore an expression of, 'God knows what new calamity has befallen the family.'"

Dissatisfied by his casual attitude but not having any choice, I walked out of the house and into the car. I called my cousin in New Jersey, USA, and asked for his opinion.

"Oh sure!" he exclaimed with certainty and self-assurance. "The ex-wife and her daughters visited me... I forget the year. The ex-wife affirmed, 'We know who it was for sure. It was the mad aunt. She's been institutionalized.'"

"No!" I blurted in consternation. "The mentally challenged aunt was given electric shocks but disclosed nothing. Her mother left compensation for members of the family who would give her asylum. Each sister has volunteered to keep her as a family member for one year."

"Oh! Is that so? I'm misinformed. I thought there was a consensus that the mad aunt stabbed her mother."

"Also, in her entire period of mental illness, there has been no hint of violence. She was a lamb. She followed her mother like a shadow. How shameful to make this helpless woman a victim."

"We'll discuss it when you come here."

I had a brief meeting with my mother's younger sister whose husband was the chief investigator.

Her comments were even briefer and articulated in a voice that suggested futility, hopelessness, and incomprehension: *Pata nahi kya hua* (Don't know what happened). *Use pakra par vo bhag gya* (We apprehended him, but he escaped)." She moved her hands in a futile gesture and looked as though she was about to weep. "*Itna dhakka laga* (We suffered an emotional push that shocked us)."

I would discuss these three responses with my mother later. In the meantime, I planned to walk in Lodi Gardens, a historic site dating to the fifteenth century and known for its stone Islamic mausoleums. The landscaped, spacious gardens, stately palm trees in columns, the man-made reservoir, and beds of sweet-smelling roses gave the gardens a lyrical dreamlike ambiance. The play of light and shadow from the sunlight filtering through the marble lattice was paradisiacal. It was a perfect escape from the mayhem of the congested city.

I found an isolated spot and settled on a bench in this green oasis. It was time to brainstorm what was what and take my findings back to my mother. I started with the premise that before examining what a person does or can execute, we must know what a person is. We must understand the ground of being before we can deduce what emerges from it.

In my experience with her and in my observation of her with family and friends, there was clearly a grandiosity and self-importance. Situations that could have been settled peaceably ended up as a test of wills in which there would be one winner. "I will get you a raise." "I can seduce your boss." "If anybody teaches Dolly to dance, it will be me." "I will show her how to make *parathas* (flatbread)." The craving for power, the struggle of wills, the one-upmanship was evident in trifling matters. True, Punjabi women as a rule have much more *chutzpah* and a robust assertiveness as compared to women of my state of Uttar Pradesh, where submissiveness is the rule. But in her case, this positive attribute was in overdrive. It was assertiveness on steroids, to use a modern day cliche. It was clearly toxic.

In combination with a pugnacious assertiveness was a Clytemnestra-like craving for power that employed manipulation to achieve its aims. The drive was unscrupulous, ruthless, and without remorse or guilt. If people dropped dead on the way, so be it. If they fail to die, kill them. It is the goal that matters, not the means. The property, assets, pension must be hers and hers alone. It was her privilege. She was entitled to it.

"I will destroy Dolly's marriage. I will teach her mother a lesson. I will poison the ears of her mother-in-law and members of the social circle. I will employ a *tantric* (black magic practitioner) to blast her life, catch her vibrations on a ring, pretend to give her the ring but retrieve it for black magic. She will die a cursed death."

Manipulative people do not understand the concept of boundaries. They are relentless in their pursuit of what they want. They feel entitled to push boundaries—a couple of corpses is a trifle matter. Murders can be outsourced; assaults can be paid off. Mad women can be blamed. Demand instant, unearned respect. If disrespected, react with the most violent intensity.

After wreaking havoc with people's lives, the aggressor spins the wheels of manipulation to inspire pity and to see her as a victim. "I have been sinned against, poor me! I was made to stand on my head. I, a proud, broad-chested *Punjabi,* was insulted by these puny *UP* idiots." With cries such as these, they evoke pity, sympathy, and compassion. They play on people to get cooperation.

The finger-pointing is blatant. It is part of their revenge dynamics. "They broke my marriage. I am without my house. They poisoned the ears of my husband." Such manipulators cheat and lie and make you feel it's your fault. They are the craftsmen of destruction. The thought of examining their own conscience does not arise. The ability or will to discriminate between right and wrong and between justice and injustice is abandoned. What is left is high-pitched, neurotic drama. All attacks are accompanied with obsessive puffs of smoke from her nicotine-stained fingers. A pack of cigarettes is her constant companion.

I finally had the courage to call a spade a spade. The facts gave me no choice. To hide behind oily and glib sentiments of honor and reputation was rank cowardice. I was at war. I planned to return to my mother's house and report my findings. My mother was on the front porch snapping beans. Her clipboard, with a sheaf of papers scribbled on in Hindi, were lying untidily on the table in front of her.

As I joined her on the porch, she put a finger vertically to her mouth to caution me to be quiet.

"Watch the sparrows and that crow," she whispered.

And indeed I witnessed a guerilla war. The crow, an old enemy hung around the wood-fortified bird cages I had brought for my mother from the Farmer's Market in Brevard, North Carolina, to safeguard her precious sparrows from predatory birds. She had affixed them within the thick branches of a vine that covered the front portion of the porch. Thick strands of this vine hung down about a foot and swayed in the breeze. The sparrows fluttered around the small, empty spaces of this greenery.

This crow was a bully, or he played at being a bully to create drama. My mother said smilingly that the crow appeared almost every day to harass the sparrows but had never succeeded. When it appeared, some twelve sparrows would unify into a guerrilla army and attack in unison. The crow would flee and sit on the wall separating the house from the street. The brisk flutter of wings and the unexpected momentum of the birds attacking in unison was enough to intimidate the crow.

"If the crow succeeds, I'm here with my cane," she said, "but my sparrows are well-equipped to protect themselves. I scatter bird feed to keep the army well fed."

"Yes," I interjected. "The army marches on its stomach."

She pulled gently at one of the creeper-like strands from the entangled, dense mass of the vine. "I got a tiny runner like this from Zurich, Switzerland, on my trip to Europe some years ago. Now look at it! It's uncontrollable. I have to get it trimmed every few months. But it serves as a cradle, a perch, and a hiding place for the sparrows. The way this vine grows reminds me of my unruly hair when I was growing up. My mother would fasten the thick strands with a slide, but they would extricate themselves and hang around my face in curls and ringlets. A hairdo of this kind was considered flirtatious, but my hair had a mind of its own. My hair was so long that I could sit on it. In those days, prospective in-laws measured the length of a woman's hair."

"I think you can sit on your hair even now. When you comb it, your arm has to stretch its full length to reach the silver tips. What would people of your generation say about my short hair or my daughter's that was cropped even closer to the head?"

"They would think you were widows. Widows shaved their hair as a sign of renunciation from physical and material pleasures."

Just then a mangy-looking cat stole across the patch of grass to a hanging swing in the corner of the rectangular garden. The swing was so heavily festooned by the creeper that it was barely visible to the eye.

"That's the cat's perch. It gave birth to six kittens on that perch. It used to keep one wary eye on me to check if I would wreck its home. But now it's comfortable. It's settled in."

"Well, don't you want to know what my brother, cousin, and aunt had to say about the murder?",

"Yes, let me finish snapping these beans and I'll be ready for the gossip. My tiny garden is a source of so much activity. I can hardly keep up!"

My mother returned from the kitchen and seated herself comfortably on the cane chair.

"So what did your brother say? What was his verdict?"

"He declared the murder to be a mystery. He did not want to pursue the subject further. He had a nauseous expression on his face. The subject is truly unpalatable to him."

My mother took a deep breath. "I know there has been a travesty of justice and much has been concealed and covered up. I can't get the policewoman's words out of my mind, 'Now it's your brother's turn to be murdered.' She had experience with murders that are motivated by inheritance issues." She put a hand through her gray hair. "If the son of a deceased woman is denying the facts, pretending that his ex-wife and he were on friendly terms, it is pointless for me to be embroiled in the case. Just call it a mystery and save yourself from exhaustion."

"Sounds like your brother was in damage control mode," I added.

"Yes, he has the future of his daughters to think about. Why destroy their lives with the poisonous gossip going around?"

"My cousin in New Jersey had no doubt about the culprit. 'Everybody knows it was the mad aunt who did it. She's been institutionalized.'"

This revelation shocked my mother. "*Kaha se kaha baat chali gai*," she said with awe in her voice.

The expression is tricky to translate. Generally, it means that the truth has moved far from its source. More accurately, it translates as a distortion so gross that it is no longer recognizable. The expression reminds me of a game in which people sit in a circle. One person whispers a statement into the ear of the one next to him or her. The second whispers the message into the ear of the second and so forth. The last one articulates what was whispered. The circle breaks out into laughter at how the message bears no resemblance to the original statement. It is a game to demonstrate the unreliable nature of gossip.

She was so deeply shocked that she was at a loss for words. "My poor sister," she moaned, "*bichari, bichari* (pathetic, pathetic)."

We were both quiet. I had my own thoughts. Any mention of Vimla was left out when family members talked about the family. They identified with the successful members—those that drove out in a Landau to receive a medal; the cousins who were tennis champions in India. My grandfather's contribution to the Theosophical Society. His friendship with Annie Besant. The gossip that Annie Besant communicated to my grandfather about her engagement to Bernard Shaw. The reasons she got disengaged. My grandmother's pampered childhood with feet shod in velvet. She walked on Persian carpets. Her clothes were as soft as damask. The maids that walked behind fanned her. The fans were described as made of a special cotton, the kind that pundits used to fan images of Krishna.

All this time, skinny, dark Vimla with bewildered eyes was walking unnoticed on the rooftop. Up and down, she walked like an automaton. I wondered how many miles she covered. She never paused or sat down to rest. Perhaps the stillness would have brought back memories of rejection. She never fell off the roof. She knew the roof had limits she must not transgress. She just walked from one end of the roof to the other end, nonstop. She went unnoticed because she was no trouble. She ate normally. She could control her bladder, but as she grew older, there were accidents. Where was the violence? She recognized her mother and laid her head on her shoulder when tired. Her mother was the only constant presence. Her sisters all married and moved out. I can't remember anybody asking for her or bringing her presents.

To pin a murder on a shadow of a woman was monstrous. That this woman who did not know who she was and had no comprehension of the furniture or the ornaments around her should stand on the sofa and remove a dagger and pierce it into her mother's heart and then lie down and fall asleep next to her was such a monstrous thought that it rocked my imagination. To use this mad woman to shield the true culprit, to make her a villain in this high drama, to spread this lie abroad to all my cousins who swallowed it readily was hard to comprehend. The murder had been conceived, designed, and stitched together by a she-devil.

Finally, my mother broke the silence, "What did Veena, my sister, have to say?"

"She said the event was incomprehensible. She made a futile gesture about the assailant escaping from the train. She looked very sad. Her eyes were troubled."

"She may not know the truth or is wearing a mask, a facade. I know my brother has blocked his heart and built an impenetrable wall to prevent the truth from seeping in. I don't think he can survive very long trying to hide from himself."

My mother got up to move into the living room. She walked like someone used to grieving, someone who had found a way to cope with her own guilt of negligence and her brother's inauthentic life. She went through the motions of walking but was not actually there. There were moments when it was better to be away from oneself. The anguish of grief could wreck one's life.

There are two more reactions that are worth recording. Both occurred in 1992, years after my grandmother's murder. In the first, my Aunt Sarla was sitting with my mother on the bed, resting her body on a pile of cushions against the wall. They were reading about a bizarre crime in the newspaper of cannibalism and expressing shock. As I passed by, my aunt caught the edge of my garment.

Raising her eyes heavenward, she said in hushed tones, "Dolly, anything can happen in life. Anything, anything!" She raised one arm in disbelief and exclaimed in an astonished voice, "Could anyone have imagined that my mother would be murdered? Do you know how she was raised? Do you know who her father was?" Her mouth fell open in total disbelief. "Anything can happen in life. Anything! There are no guarantees." She let my garment go but remained in a state of shock for some time. Five years had passed, but she still was unable to accept the existential happening.

The second is my elder brother's response. He had been estranged from the entire family and all that transpired in the family since 1972.

At a chance meeting in Montreal, he asked me, "How is *naniji*?"

I could tell that he expected the commonplace response of her suffering from gout and other ailments that go with senility. But he was not ready for what he heard.

"She was murdered," I said bluntly.

"WHAT? WHAT?" he whispered breathlessly.

I had never seen his eyes roll as they did.

"WHAT? HOW? WHY?"

CHAPTER 14

A Contrast and Conclusion

The world is an evil place. Not because of the people who are evil but because of the people who don't do anything about it.
—Albert Einstein

We were up with the sunrise and the sparrows. My mother was wearing one of her finely textured, lightweight saris that ballooned like an opening parachute when a gust of wind swept through her precious garden. The sparrows were pecking at their cereal, and the glacial aqua boulders glistened with a gold sheen from the early morning rays striking the surface. It was a blessed sunrise that inspired my mother to visit the Lotus Temple for restoration of her bruised spirit.

The Lotus Temple, often described as "the modern Taj Mahal," was the most visited architectural marvel in the world. My mother felt that its graceful beauty would bury all the demons that had been released in the psyche from the endless chatter of my grandmother's murder.

The lotus itself was highly metaphorical. Its roots were buried in mud, darkness, and debris. In its nascent state, its tender roots battled insects, fish, and bugs to survive.

Despite the debris and darkness, the stem pushed upward even though no light was visible. Finally, after battling the darkness, the elements, and the insects, it emerged triumphant into the light. It was emblematic of human struggle that must battle the dark forces,

the demonic passions, and the negative elements to reach enlighten-
ment: the flowering of the thousand-petaled lotus at the crown of
the head.

When I expressed skepticism at the possibility of such a trium-
phal ascension of spiritual forces, my mother gave me an intense look
and exclaimed, "*Amma ji*, your paternal grandmother, died in lotus
pose. *Rigor mortis* set in which rigidified her body into a statue-like
Buddha. The cot on which she was seated was carried by four of her
devotees into the streets to announce, 'If you doubted this woman
was a saint, here is the proof. Her life exited from the roof of her
head.' Her corpse, still sitting upright in lotus pose, was covered with
jasmine flowers and marigolds, lifted and seated on a raft that floated
on the strong current of the river Ganges.

"I was her daughter-in-law and witnessed her death. At the
moment of her death, she hoisted her body up to a sitting position,
got into lotus pose, said, 'Oм,' and died. I could see her body floating
on the raft in a sitting position for a long time. It finally looked like a
speck of orange, but it was still seated, and the raft was still moving."

One grandmother stabbed with a dagger, the other seated like
the Buddha and sailing triumphantly down the Ganges. The contrast
was staggering. I was also aware that the pampered princess with feet
shod in velvet was not religious. She was proud of the Lucknow Club
membership she promoted. She was proud of her ancestral anteced-
ents. By contrast, Amma, my paternal grandmother, was a widow
who struggled with all the privations of a woman alone in the world
with some five sons to raise. Still, she fought to fulfill her responsibilities and, in old age, established an asylum for widows like herself.

Early in life, she renounced the world, seeking total detachment
from the worldly life.

"Was your mother at all religious? Most of the women in her
time were temple-goers," I asked. I had never seen a prayer room in
her house.

"No," my mother answered, "her orientation was not religious.
I would call her a *mamuli* (ordinary, commonplace) practitioner.
She enjoyed reading the epic *The Ramayana* but never ventured into
the philosophical understanding of spirituality as described in *The*

Upanishads and the systems of meditation. By contrast, your Amma never let go of her rosary. She never postponed or skipped her practice of meditation, even if there was a death in the family. It is dedication of this kind that gave her detachment from earthly matters. At the moment of death, she could let go of all creature comforts and all human connections."

On one of my visits, I could recall my mother castigating my grandmother for worrying and creating anxiety in everyone instead of saying God's name. She answered sheepishly that she wanted to find consolation in God, but His name would not come to her lips.

My mother turned to me and said, "Did you hear that? The lesson is if you do not say God's name all your life, you cannot say it at the moment of death. Your life is a preparation for death. Your last thought is the essence of how you have lived. It will determine your next birth. So pray constantly."

We were approached by a charming Iranian girl who wished to be our guide. She told us that the Bahai were persecuted in Iran and so had left Iran to find shelter in India.

"We can't pursue higher education and our houses can be raided anytime."

As we approached the lotus structure, she pointed out that there were nine entrances to the temple, nine pools of water surrounding the structure, and twenty-seven independent marble petals, which clustered in groups of three to form nine sides.

I remembered that the number nine occurred forty-three times in the *Bible* and that Jesus died in the ninth hour to redeem the world, which would then start fresh with no one. There were 360 degrees in a circle; the digits added up to nine. If cut in a semicircle of 180 degrees, the digits would again add up to nine. If cut into quarters of ninety degrees, the nine was again present. I had read somewhere that numbers were not invented, they were discovered. Our guide endorsed that theory. She said the number nine was inherent in the very structure of the temple. The number symbolized completeness, faith, universality, love, charity, and more. She related quaint facts to back up the hypothesis. I remembered that my Amma fasted for nine days to commemorate the nine faces of the goddess. There was also a temple of *navagraha* (nine planets).

We entered the spacious center of the interior of the lotus. Services could be held in all religions and all denominations. We learned that the founder was jailed, tortured, and ultimately crucified for rejecting fundamentalist Islam and espousing tolerance and universality of belief. The Islamic world could not endure the switch from singularity to plurality.

My mother wanted to return to the garden and enjoy the umbrella-like trees that had hundreds of mandarin oranges dotting them like tiny orange stars. We sat on one of the stone benches to continue our conversation.

"Amma," she said, "did not suffer fools gladly."

She related an incident that took place in Allahabad, the town where the Ganges and the Jumna meet. One early morning, she took a bicycle *rickshaw* to take a dip in the Ganges. She wore the orange robe of a renunciate and held her heavy wooden staff in one hand, striking the ground firmly as she walked briskly to mount the rickshaw. The driver started pedaling but muttered something vulgar about her womanhood. She told him to stop the *rickshaw*, alighted without his help, raised her *lathi* (staff), and whacked him hard on the head. Then seating herself comfortably on the seat, she ordered, "*Ab chal* (now move)."

There were other incidents of a similar kind. She requested her cook to shave his mustache in case a stray hair might drop into the lentil soup and pollute the food. When he refused, she took a burning log out of the *choolah* (stove made of clay and bricks) and set half of his mustache on fire. The surviving right side, he shaved himself. She had also thrashed a "holy man" who had attempted to gain sexual favors from a young widow. When she reported the indecency, she thrashed the man and chased him out of the building onto the street. A dozen bald-headed widows with staffs raised joined her. The man ran, covering his bruised head with his hands.

The feminists would have loved her, I thought.

My maternal grandmother was a lady. Her speech was cultivated, and her choice of clothes were tasteful. She matched her silks.

Her writing style was literary. But she was unable to hold her own against the forces of chaos. She spoke quietly, expressing her fears in whispers. By contrast, my paternal grandmother was blunt, assertive, loud, and made nothing of using physical force. Nobody could stand up to her. She symbolized righteous wrath. The kind of power that *Durga*, the goddess of war, confers on her worshippers.

I felt like walking to the end of the lawn and occupying a seat that would give us a view of the red sandstone that outlined the paths and the flower beds. They gave the lawns a geometric grace. My mother agreed and we sauntered toward the gallery and the library.

"Your Amma walked briskly, none of us could keep up with her."

"How did she raise her children?" I asked, "Was she equally hard on them?"

"She was no kinder to her children. When she caught your father, her son, eating sardines in secret, she followed the trail of the stinking sardines to his hiding place. She hurled the can out the window and howled in a loud voice for all inmates to hear, 'If the White man canned his shit, you would eat it.' Her politics was conservative, 'What's all this noise about Gandhi? All he's done is to hoist latrine cleaners on our heads.' She would lash out and strip the hypocrisy and oily, glib lies off anyone, irrespective of gender, rank, class, or caste."

I took a deep breath. What an anomaly Amma was for her time. Widows were throwing themselves on the funeral pyres of their husbands. She looked like someone who could push both the husband and the presiding priests into the fire. I had heard she had walked to Mansarovar as an older woman in her late sixties. Mansarovar, at 15,060 feet above sea level, is the world's highest high-water lake. She had walked there twice. It is a pilgrimage center holy to Lord Shiva. The trek is so formidable that not everybody returns alive.

Another young Iranian woman joined us. Did we have any questions? she inquired. I asked her if the marble was native or from abroad. She said it was from a mountain in Greece. I asked about the location of other Bahai Temples. She answered there were seven in all and a fourth under construction. They were located on seven continents. The eighth that was under construction was in Chile. In photographs, it featured torqued steel wings and was nestled in the rolling topography of the mountains and surrounded by reflecting pools. I assumed that nine would be the final number.

In a congested, overpopulated city such as Delhi, green spaces that were scattered in all neighborhoods had the refreshing quality of an oasis in an urban desert. They provided an opportunity to step out of mercantile haggling, relax under trees, read a newspaper in silence, and simply reflect. They were analogous to the lungs of a city. I thought of Pascal's words, "Be still and know that I am God."

The Iranian tourist guide departed to help other groups of people, I turned to my mother with a question that had been bothering me. "Ayn Rand, a popular but controversial American novelist who had lived in the Soviet Union for a major portion of her life, was of the opinion that evil requires the sanction of the victim. This would mean that my grandmother was somehow complicit in her murder. For example, if Amma had been in her place, she would not have whispered her fears to family but confronted the estranged wife with: 'Hey you with the wicked eyes! What devious scheme are you concocting? If I see you coming down those stairs again, I'll whack you one and have you run out of town.' Amma practiced Albert Camus's cynical counsel: 'There is no fate that cannot be surmounted by scorn.'"

My mother laughed. She would have done more, gone up the stairs, and flung her clothes out of the room. The woman would have been terrorized out of her wits. Amma would have turned the aggressor into a victim. I've always said that common sense and pragmatic action is with the uneducated or the minimally literate. Their instincts dictate their actions. Education, especially higher education, somehow declaws a person. It muddles and weakens the mind with too many points of view.

"We become Hamlet-like, rationalizing, reflecting, philosophizing, lost in words, and incapable of focused, palpable action. In this sense, character is destiny," I reflected.

"But in Amma's case, the authority, the strength of character, the energy, the fearlessness was a by-product of her spiritual discipline. Her disciplined hours of meditation over more than three decades had sharpened her faculties to a razor's edge. She was self-realized. God was manifest in her. For an elderly woman to reject all help with a 'Get out. Don't you dare compromise my last moment of death,' to sit up, get into perfect lotus position, say her final sacred *mantra*, 'Om,' the primordial sound and give up her breath is an act of will that is superhuman. It is this will that she had strengthened in the likeness of an elephant carrying a heavier and heavier load, or a weightlifter increasing his weights over decades of practice."

My mother did not have this Kali-like, all-consuming brilliance. She was born into a privileged existence. She felt she was entitled to a comfortable life. She had never confronted a life-threatening situation. Amma, on the other hand, confronted life-threatening situations on a daily basis. She and her cohort of bald widows had been hardened in the bowels of hell. But Amma alone had transmuted that dross into gold. She had overcome; she had transcended.

With that verdict, I felt my mother had closed the subject for good. We had literally rehashed the event to death. Her conclusion was that humans were at different levels of evolution and till such time that the darkness within had not been made conscious to the light, we would remain the playthings of *karma* or fate to murder and be murdered. The enormity of the injustice might baffle us, but it was simply part of the learning process for both aggressor and victim.

We now walked to the gallery and the library. The presence of books never failed to remind me of my father. He was never without a book on philosophy and shared his prose gems with us over breakfast. He died in 1972 and had lived through the most turbulent saga of the divorce of his brother-in-law.

On one occasion, when I was standing on the veranda of our Agra house, I witnessed a scene that stayed with me. My father reclining in a cane chair reading, a troubled man touching his feet and frantically pleading with him. Dropping his book, my father tried to raise the anxious man with both his hands. I could tell he was trying to calm him with conciliatory words.

My mother explained the man on his knees was the brother of the estranged wife. He was begging my father to withdraw the case that would leave his sister divorced and mostly helpless. He had approached my father because my father was responsible for resolving the legal issues in the case. The man was pleading on his sister's behalf.

Later in the day, my father exchanged information with my mother. His face was saddened, and his eyes looked troubled. He had always played the role of protector of widows and of women in trouble, always going out of his way to fight their legal battles at no cost. But in this family matter, he was playing a role less than benevolent.

He was spared the news of my grandmother's murder in '87. He passed away in '72.

We walked through the picture gallery of the founder's life. The fading brown and cream photographs at the entrance showed crowds of people attracted by his benevolent message, but the final photographs were chilling in their content. The orthodox saw him as a threat. His message of tolerance and peace was too radical for an eye-for-an-eye theology. So they tortured him and hanged him. He was killed as was Martin Luther King, as was Gandhi, as was Jesus. It was imperative that the truth be nailed so that the lie could live.

We left the grounds refreshed but thoughtful. My mother's *Fiat* swept into the driveway.

I walked onto the front porch. The crow was perched on the wall. Some dozen sparrows were hiding in the twisted coils of the creeper in readiness to defend their lives and their fortifications. I had to smile at the cosmic drama being played out in my mother's tiny garden. As long as the weak could band together to fight the forces of darkness, there was hope for the world.

CHAPTER 15

Endings

My uncle passed away in 1989. He was visiting my cousin in New Jersey, who stepped to get a cigarette package from the vending machine outside the apartment. When he returned, he found my uncle doubled up in pain. He was rushed to emergency, where he died of his fourth heart attack.

His ex-wife died some years later in New Delhi. On account of familial acrimony, the cause of her death is uncertain. Rumor has it that she was uncomfortable in the house after my grandmother's death and was moved to an independent apartment by her daughters. She breathed her last in that house. My mother believes that she died of a bad conscience and mental trauma.

"I can tell you this," she said, closing her fingers tightly. "Your grandmother's ghost will not spare her. Your grandmother was a tenacious woman in life, and she will be tenacious in death."

My mother died peacefully in 2018. Some hours before her death, she asked to be seated on the front porch. Her corpse wrapped in white sheets was moved across the porch, past the hanging creeper and the bird houses into the van that transported it to the cremation grounds.

Vimla was given lodging with each sister in turn and compensated monetarily with the money my grandmother had arranged for her well-being. Sarla lodged her for eight years. The youngest daughter was unable or unwilling to house her sister and confined her to a mental asylum. The authorities reported that she would often repeat the following in a singsong in Hindi: "Sarla, if I cannot come to you, surely, you can come to me." On one of my trips to India, I wanted to visit her with presents. My mother reported that she had passed away. She could not remember any details. She was invisible in life and in death.

This book is dedicated to Vimla—to give her visibility and to exonerate her of all wrongdoing.

Het Ram, my great grandfather

My great grandmother

Raj Rani, my grandmother

Raj Rani, my grandmother

Raj Rani, my grandmother

Ram Gopal, my grandfather

From left to right: My uncle, my mother, my father

My mother with her children. I'm standing on the right.

My uncle as a young man

My uncle on his marriage day

My aunt, the prime suspect

ABOUT THE AUTHOR

Photo credit: Saronda Morgan

Dr. Eira Patnaik received her BA and MA degrees from Allahabad University, Allahabad, India, in 1962 and 1964. She attained first division and was awarded six gold medals for achieving the highest marks in English literature. Subsequently, she received a doctorate of arts from Syracuse University, Syracuse, New York, in 1980. She was appointed professor of English at Frostburg State University, Frostburg, Maryland, in 1973 and retired professor emeritus in 2001. Her distinctions include *National Endowment of the Humanities* grants to the Universities of Georgetown, Stanford, Cornell, Duke, Amherst, and a yearlong research grant that she completed at Berkeley University. Eira has received the CICHE Faculty Grant to demonstrate the literary fertilization between India and the United States. In addition, the Maryland Humanities Council, Speaker's Bureau, selected her as storyteller and public speaker for the State of Maryland from 1999 to 2001. She has delivered academic papers at the Universities of Boston, West Chester, Illinois, Virginia, Maryland, Towson, to name a few. She was also appointed by the University of Pittsburgh for their Seminar at Sea program to teach on board of ship while sailing around the world for one hundred days. She has traveled to over fifty-five countries.

Although based in the US since 1970, Eira is familiar with conditions in India, especially in New Delhi. Her familiarity can be attributed to a particular circumstance: In order to provide company to her ageing mother who lived in Greater Kailash 1, Eira made several extended trips to India. During these trips, her mother familiarized her with the illustrious history of the family. In addition, she also visited her aged grandmother and her mentally challenged aunt, both of whom lived in an upscale neighborhood but, despite the comfortable environment, were largely isolated and lonesome.

Her memoir is a truthful narrative of what she observed and what was disclosed to her by her mother and some members of the family. It is not a work of the imagination.

Eira's other interests are a love of the classical Argentine tango. Her skills in the dance were acquired by the painstaking effort of Jim Curtis, her instructor, and were honed by experience acquired on dozens of trips to Buenos Aires, Argentina. After Eira received the equivalent of a master's degree in the Argentine tango from the Dance Academy in Buenos Aires, Jim and Eira gave classes on the tango for several years in their studio in Brevard, North Carolina.

Eira can be reached at patnaik.eira@gmail.com.

Lightning Source UK Ltd.
Milton Keynes UK
UKHW010905080223
416610UK00013B/808

9 781685 260460